THE GIFT
OF TOMORROW

Anita Schneider

ISBN 978-1-950647-70-5

Cover image: Can Stock Photo / Alinamd

Publishing assistance by BookCrafters, Parker, Colorado.
www.bookcrafters.net

TABLE OF CONTENTS

Chapter One

THE BEGINNING

December 2014 seemed to be the same as any other December, Thanksgiving was over, the Christmas tree was up, the Nativity scene was in place, the weather outside was cold and windy. Seemed normal to me. I had a cough, and even that was normal, after all it was December and a cough is normal for that time of the year.

The crazy cough just kept hanging on, so one day when I was at work at Gibson Healthmart Drug store, I asked the Pharmacist if she had anything to help me get rid of this crazy cough. She suggested a couple things that I should try and if that does not seem to help, maybe I should see a doctor. Well I thought I would give the over-the-counter products a try, after all I did not have a fever and my lungs didn't hurt when I took a deep breath, just this crazy cough. Two weeks later I still had this nagging cough, but it was getting close to Christmas and I thought I would wait until after the first of the year to go to the doctor. I still had a lot of things to do to get ready for Christmas.

Christmas came and it was wonderful, all the family was here and little Delaney, our youngest granddaughter was a year and a half, so she made it special. The excitement and love that a little one brings to Christmas makes it so meaningful. The oldest grandson Clayton is such a neat kid, he was on the floor helping the little ones get their toys set up, and he showed them how things work.

As I grow older, I think I need to turn the holidays over to one of my daughters-in-law, but my boys seem to think that is just is not Christmas if they don't come home, so home it is. Joshua, our youngest son, and his family usually stay a few days after Christmas, since they come from Kansas City and we do not get to see then that often, and this year is no different. Over the next couple days my cough seemed to get more nagging and deeper, so Joshua insisted I see the doctor. So I guessed that was what I should do. He works in a hospital and I respect his judgment and promised that I would go.

January 2015, I called the medical clinic and set up an appointment with Lisa, the Physician's Assistant. She checked things out and did not think I had pneumonia, but to be sure she ordered an X-ray just in case she missed something. She ordered a couple of prescriptions for my cough and said if not better in a few days to call her back. I had the X-ray done and headed down to Gibson's for my medicine and of course chat with the girls. Gibson's has this quaint little soda fountain that was built in the 1920s, so we sat at the bar having a cup of coffee and my phone rings. I answered it, the voice on the other end says, "Anita, this is Lisa and you are right, I do not find any evidence of pneumonia, but I see something I want to clarify. I would like you to come back to the hospital and have a CT (computed tomography)."

I said, "No problem I'll be right up," thinking to myself, *That's weird that Lisa would call me instead of her nurse.* I made my purchases and headed to the hospital for the CT. I then went home to wait on the results.

After supper my phone rang, when I answered it, the voice on the other end said, "Anita, this is Lisa, and I am about 99% sure you have lung cancer. I have set up a couple of appointments for you, one with a Pulmonologist, and one with an Oncologist. Don't miss them. Their offices should call you next week to confirm."

Wow, I never thought I would hear those words—"you have

cancer— you have cancer." I kind of felt like I had been hit with a baseball bat, but I kept thinking, *It has not been confirmed yet. I kept thinking It cannot be true, it just can't. What am I going to do, what is going to happen?* These were three of the hardest words I have ever heard, and they were said to me.

Monday morning the Pulmonologist's office called and the soonest they could get me in was next week. Boy what a long week that was, one just cannot stop their mind from thinking the worst. Next week finally came and my husband David and I headed to Hays to see this new doctor. The WaKeeney clinic had sent my scans to this doctor, he read them, and we talked about what was going on. He told me not to be so sure this scan was correct. He needed to do his tests to be sure, so he scheduled me for a scope biopsy the next week at the Hays Medical Center.

Another week of mind wondering, worrying, but I kept telling myself that the Pulmonologist did say it has not been confirmed —yet. I kept hanging on to that thought. The day finally came, and we headed to Hays with positive thoughts. I checked into the hospital for the procedure. The nurses did the work up, and then I was in the procedure room where the doctor put a scope down my throat to get a sample of the tumor that was putting pressure on my bronchus.

That was why I had a terrible cough. The tumor was so large it was putting pressure on my bronchus and obstructing my airway, so my body was trying to expel the obstruction by coughing. I coughed so hard that I bruised by ribs and even caused myself to vomit on occasion. The procedure didn't take very long, but it sure made me uncomfortable. I coughed even harder than before and my throat was sore, but I thought it was done and would find out for sure in a few days what we were looking at.

When the doctor came in and asked how I was doing, I told him about my pain, and he asked if I could take pain killers. I said I was allergic to a lot of them. He asked about Fentanyl, and I said that I had never used it, so he prescribed Fentanyl patches for my pain. A couple days later I received a call from the doctor's nurse who informed me that the procedure was not a success, as they did not retrieve any samples at all. I would have to either come in to visit with the doctor who did the procedure or talk to my regular doctor and decide where to go from here.

I chose to talk to my regular doctor instead of the not-so-professional Pulmonologist. I really did not like the guy, and he was very unprofessional and weird. After talking with my doctor, we decided a cardiovascular surgeon was the way to be assured of a biopsy so we could find out what the heck was growing inside my lung.

Dr. Ashworth, the cardiovascular surgeon's office called the next day and set up an appointment for me to meet with her next week. Great, I thought, another week of not knowing. I kept thinking *Lung cancer was the cancer people got from smoking, well I don't smoke so they must be wrong, and they just have to be wrong. Lung cancer, it just can't be, I don't understand how I could get it. I try to take care of myself and be healthy, exercise, watch what I eat, but lung cancer? It's just not possible.*

The appointment day with Dr. Ashworth finally arrived. She was a super nice person, and she assured me that she would do whatever she had to do to find out what kind of mass I had. I asked her if she could remove it, would she remove it. She assured me she would do all she could to help me. Here we go again, the biopsy date was set up for next week. Next week, next week. I am just beginning to hate those two words, next week. Don't those people know that this thing that I have is growing inside me, and they just keep saying that it will be next week. I don't mean to complain, but every time they are going to do something, it is always next week, and I have another week of wonder and worry. I do have to say that the Fentanyl patches helped with the pain, I just had to be careful and not become addicted.

Biopsy day finally came. I checked into the hospital and nurses did the preparation for my surgery. Dr. Ashworth came to let me know that the time had come to find out what was going on; an inch to two inch incision would be made and she would go into the spot and pull some samples that would be tested. Coming up from surgery was quite easy, I only feel a little sleepy and not in much pain at all. I'm sure the patches had something to do with that.

They took me to my room and later that evening the doctor came in to see me and how things were going. I asked her if she could remove the mass and she said that there was no way she could, as it was totally involved with my major arteries and there was no way to remove it. The test results would take a few days and she would call the Oncology office to have them set up a time to see me. *Oh dear*—I thought, *she is sending me to the Oncologist, and I know what that means without her saying anything else.*

The day after my surgery, two friends, Pat and Elaine came to see me in the hospital, and we played cards in the family room that evening. We played "Hand and Foot" and it was a lot of fun and took my mind off the near future. It was so nice to do something besides think the surgery, the biopsy and the results of the biopsy, and what was going to happen next. The day before I left a couple other friends Bernita and Ranita stopped by, we played cards also. I was feeling fairly good and we laughed a lot. The family room was really nice and had a lot of things for the families to do, free drinks, puzzles, cards and books to read. There were comfortable sitting areas, and nice tables and chairs to play cards and things.

My stay in the hospital was five days, but it wasn't a bad thing. The little incision turned out to be right at six inches and the drain tube in my chest was a new experience for me. When Dr. Ashworth pulled it out she said to take a deep breath and wow—I think she pulled part of my bottom lip out with the tube. Not really, but it did hurt a bit, however everything was fine, and I would be able to go home.

Yes, home with my wondering thoughts, my mind playing

what ifs, how long, and what will the future have in store for me. Will I be able to handle the treatment, the stress on my body, the loss of my hair? I just did not know what to expect.

Chapter Two

THE PREPARATION

Think positively—beginning with the moment you wake up.

The week I arrived home, the Oncologist office called me to set up an appointment for, you guessed it, next week. At this time, I knew it was not good news, so I felt I needed to tell my family. I called the boys and told them that I had cancer and was going to see the Oncologist to find out where we would go from here. If they wanted to go with me, to ask questions and be there for support, they sure could.

I was so scared. I didn't have a clue what was going to happen, I just kept thinking the worst: *chemotherapy, radiation, no surgery, too big and involved with my main arteries, obstructing my airway and only God knows what else was going on inside. It was already March, and I started this in January. How much bigger is that tumor now compared to what it was, how long have I had this thing growing,* my mind just could not stop wondering.

The day for our first meeting with the Oncologist came and all my boys were going to be there with me; Jason, our oldest, Jeremy, second son, Joshua, our youngest, and of course my husband David. The daughters-in-law and my sisters were also there but waited in the waiting room. Dr. O'Dea was the Oncologist, and she seemed nice and caring. She began by telling us that the mass was definitely cancer, Adenocarcinoma, which is non-small cell lung cancer, the kind that non-smokers get, and it is the most controllable kind of lung cancer. The first thing we will do is an MRI, (magnetic resonance imaging) to get a better look at the mass itself. We will then schedule a PET scan, (positron emission tomography) to find out where and what is all involved with this cancer. You see when you have a PET scan, they inject radioactive dye into you blood stream and it shows all the active cancer cells as little green critters.

She asked if there were any questions, and Joshua had a few and they were answered, and everyone seemed pleased with what she had to say. I asked if she had any idea what kind of procedure she was planning. She said that it would probably be a regiment of chemotherapy and radiation because they work better together than separate, it was harder on the patient but this kind of cancer is very hard to get ahead of. She thought this was the best way to start the long process. It was not going to be an easy road, but she felt it was the best method of treatment, and I was strong enough to handle it. The Fentanyl patches should help with the pain if I continued to use them. Wow, that was a lot of information to be given is such a short time, especially to someone who knows nothing about cancer. She suggested I write down any questions so we could address them at our next visit.

The boys were the first ones to go out into the waiting room, and my sister JoAnn knew the news was not good by the look on Jeremy's face. She said her heart just sank and wanted to cry, but felt she had to keep a strong appearance for the boys. They all waited for me to come into the area before they started to talk about what we found out. I told them what I knew and asked them to please keep me in their prayers, as it was going to be a long hard road.

The hospital called to schedule my MRI for the next week, and the week after that the PET Scan. So here we go again-- another couple weeks for those thoughts to roll again about this new thing I had growing inside my lung. Cancer is one of the scariest things I have ever thought of, not alone have growing in my lung. *Will I be able to fight it, will it get the best of me? Pain, suffering and I just know, I'll lose my hair, everyone that has chemo loses their hair. Seems like a small thing if it will get rid of the tumor, but I will look like a bald man. What will people say, how will they act toward me?* Just so many unanswered questions and feelings that my mind would not let alone.

The day came for the MRI-- not a big deal, I've had one before, but I just don't like being stuck into that little tube. *It gets me so claustrophobic, can I stay still for that long without coughing? What if I start to cough and not be able to sit up and get it to stop?* I said something to the nurse as she was getting me ready, and she assured me not to worry, if they needed to pull me out, they would. I was just to try my best to take my mind off what is going on. They put a small pair of goggles on me that showed a television show to distract me from what was going on and hopefully get me to relax. To my surprise it worked, it was kind of hard to hold my breath without coughing but I managed to do it. When I could take a deep breath, I did and swallowed hard to help me not to cough.

I wondered why they had to wait a week between scans, so I asked. The reason they had to wait was so the dye injected into my veins had time to be eliminated out of my body through the kidneys, and that is really hard on kidneys that are a little older, as mine are. That made sense to me, so I just had to wait it out again. The week went by quite rapidly, but the whole situation was kind of running its course on me.

I felt really depressed, my color was pail, no twinkle in my eyes. I'm sure the reason I felt like that was because of the unknown and the busy thoughts roaming around in my head. I think one of the scariest things is the unknown, if you know what is going to happen, you can deal with it a lot better. It was hard for me to smile, and that is so unlike me. I usually had a smile on my face and a happy hello or kind word to everyone I met. I decided to do a little research on the good ole computer and find out more about the treatment that I was about to start. I know you can't believe everything you read on the internet, but it can definitely give you an idea what to expect. The thing that stuck in my head after reading page after page, was the impact the power of positive thinking has on the outcome. That put a whole new aspect on my attitude, I was going to try to keep a positive spin on my life. I took many a deep breath and tried to put a smile on my face when I met someone or talked to a friend on the phone. I kept telling myself I can do this. I can beat this monster inside me.

Time for the PET scan, I had really no idea what to expect since I haven't had one before. First thing they do is inject radioactive stuff in your veins and then you wait for a few minutes for it to overrun your whole body, which was kind of scary to me, radioactive stuff in my veins. People who handle this stuff take precautions not to get it on their bodies, and they are injecting it into mine. They assured me it was safe, and it would leave through the kidneys if I drank a lot of water for the next few days. Boy, did I drink, and drink.

Middle of March arrived, and David, Mari and I sat in the Oncologist office waiting to find out what was going to be next, and what was going to happen to me. I was really scared, I know I wanted to get things started, but now that the time was growing near, I trembled with fear, my heart was pounding, and the unknown was so very scary. Big sigh--they just called my name to see Dr. O'Dea. I go with David and Mari by my side and sit in the exam room, temperature is normal, blood pressure is unbelievably normal for all the anxiety I feel. When the doctor came in, with my heart pounding in my chest, I calmly said, "Well what is the verdict?"

She said, "All the tests confirmed what we originally thought. The tumor is approximately the size of a baseball, but I think we can treat it successfully. There are also a few cancer spots down the sternum. So since the cancer has some cells outside the lung we will call you in stage two at this point. This is what I want to do. I'll have Dr. Cunningham's office give you a call to set up an appointment to have a port put in your chest on the right side. We'll have the Radiation department call to coordinate with you to make your body mold for your radiation treatment. Once this is completed, I will set up the time for you to start your treatment. You will have a radiation treatment, which should only take about fifteen minutes. You will then check in and get ready for your chemotherapy; each day will take a different amount of time. We will have you do this every day for six weeks except for Saturdays and Sundays, those are days to catch your breath and get ready for another full week of treatments."

Okay, deep breath, time to start the long road of treatment so I can get back to a type of normality or at least my new normal, which was kind of scary since I really did not know what that would be. Doctors always ask if you have any questions. Well I didn't know much about what was going to happen or what to expect, so I didn't know what to ask, but I guessed I would learn.

Sure enough, Dr. Cunningham's office called, and we set up an appointment for next week. Not really knowing much about a port, I had to look it up. A chemotherapy port, sometimes referred to as a mediport, cancer port, or portacath, is a vascular access device that is implanted under the skin so that people with cancer can be given chemotherapy. A power port is a port that enables patients to receive IV therapy as well as contrast CT scans, and take blood. Knowing what it was, I could tell the doctor which kind I wanted him to put in, of course I wanted the power port so it could be used for other infusions and not just chemo. That procedure was a piece of cake, pretty much an in and out. I went to sleep, I woke up and as soon as I could eat and drink, I was good to go. The nurse told me she would let the radiology department know that my surgery was completed and ready for the mold to be made.

The radiation department called and told me we could make my mold the next week. Well, here I go again, a week of uncontrollable thoughts, the nighttime was the worst, my mind just wondered about everything that was going on, so of course my sleep was minimal. *Why can't I think of these things when I am in the doctor's office? Maybe I don't want her to think I am stupid or non-trusting, I don't know, there are so many unknown things rolling around in my head, I just don't know where to start.*

I was sitting at home waiting and my phone rings. It was my friend Wanda, and she would like to come to my house to talk. Wanda has had cancer for probably three years, and she knows how I must feel. She would like to help me to understand what is going to happen and answer some of my questions. She was God-sent, she made me feel comfortable and answered some of the unknown things I worried about. I felt at ease with her since we have been friends for a long time, and she knew how I was feeling with all the thoughts and worries. Three hours went by so fast, and she made me feel better about things. So now I was ready for the fight of my life, even though everybody's reaction to the treatment can be different, in many ways they are the same. Someone to talk to was such a help, and she put me somewhat at ease.

The time came to make the body mold for radiation, and I had no clue what that really was. I checked in at the hospital, and a nurse from the radiology department came and called me back. She said we would go into the CT scanning room, I lay on a bag filled with Styrofoam pellets, and they pushed me into the CT scanner. When they got the exact area where the tumor was they put a tattoo spot and withdrew all the air out of the bag so it made a mold of my upper body. That way, each time I had a radiation treatment my position would be the same and they used the tattoo to be sure they radiated the same spot each time. That made sense to me, and it was the only procedure I had done with absolutely no pain involved.

The last week of March came, and the new radiation machine was late arriving. The doctor did not want to start on the old machine, he would rather wait a week for the new one to be set up, which we did. What was one more week, these last few months everything was next week, so why not the start of treatment.

I hadn't even started treatment yet and the people in my hometown already knew what was going on. That is not always a bad thing, I started to get a lot of cards wishing me well, a speedy recovery, and most of them were sending their prayers. One can never get too many people praying for them. I will never turn down a prayer. The power of prayers is strong, and I do believe that the more support and prayers one receives, the better chance of recovery one has.

I am on Facebook and there were a lot of posts wishing me well and prayers being sent. I thought I would post my version as to what was going on in my life. I wanted the truth out there, rather than whatever anyone else said, just in case it was not the truth. I posted what I knew for sure, what was going on. I was the National FFA Alumni President, and I have a lot of friends from other states, who I also wanted to know what was going on. Within twenty-four hours I had people praying for me and wishing me well from thirty-four different states. That is a lot of prayers and I knew I could certainly use every one of them, for this cancer road I was on was going to be a rough one.

The unknown was just so scary, I just didn't know what the future would hold for me. I just put my health into the hands of the Lord and prayed for the best, I knew with His help I would get through this. What more does one need? The Lord, a great family, good friends, competent doctors, nurses and a positive attitude.

I decided I would try to keep David's life as normal as possible. Just because my life was never going to be the same, doesn't mean that his had to be in such a turmoil. He was with me every step of the way, and now that I had to go to treatment every day, I felt he should be able to do the things he needed to do, not just haul me around. Life goes on, so I guessed I had to do what I had to do and not force David into always being there. Let him do what he needed to do also.

Chapter Three

TREATMENT

*Make decisions today and don't continue
to look back at what could have been.*

My sister Mari decided to stay with us while I was in treatment. She said she could take me to treatments, cook, be my nurse, be sure I followed directions, and do what needed to be done. As it turned out she became invaluable to me, she was God sent. I tried to share with her what all was going to happen, as much as I knew, but of course it was the blind leading the blind. As it turned out, Mari was the question asking queen, if she didn't know what was going on, she asked and made sure she knew what to do or how to make sure things were done right at home.

Monday, April 1, 2015 and it was no April fool, and we were heading to Hays for my first treatments. First was the radiation, and the nurse called me to come back with her. We went into a room with this huge machine. I went behind a screen and took off my clothes above the waist, tucked a hand towel over my breasts, and went into the room with the huge machine. The nurse brought out the body form we made, laid it on the table under the huge machine and told me to lay on the form just like I did when they made it. When I was ready, they began to move the machine around me, it would stop and a buzz sound was made, then they would move it again, and it made the buzzing sound again. Not much to it, so it seemed, one can't see from the outside what the radiation is doing inside, but it sure didn't take very long. I then got dressed and headed out to the waiting room where Mari was waiting for me. As the nurse and I were walking out, she pointed out a basket filled with snacks if I needed one. I was welcome to anything in this basket and there was also a basket of small tubes of Aquaphor in case I felt like I was getting a burn from the radiation. Many times, people get burns at the site of the radiation or on the backside of the body. Whew, one down and only twenty-nine to go.

We then headed to the other end of the room and checked in on the Chemotherapy side of the cancer center. It wasn't long and they called me back to start my treatment, we walked into a room. There were small treatment areas with curtains dividing them, all around the outside of the room, where the treatments are given. They took me to the scale and to weigh me, then proceeded to the treatment area. There was a reclining chair like the ones used at the doctor's office, not a living room type recliner. I sat in the chair, they took my vitals, hooked me up to the blood pressure machine, cleaned my port area, inserted the needle and started me on a pre-infusion flush, and ordered my chemotherapy from the lab.

My nurse, Sara, was super nice. She saw that I was a Schneider from WaKeeney and asked if I knew Jeremy Schneider. I said he was my son. Come to find out her husband Shawn and Jeremy are really good friends and spent a lot of deer hunting seasons at my house. The chemo arrived and all the numbers were checked by Sara and another nurse to be sure things are correct. Then Sara put on a waterproof gown and double gloves and began my chemo treatment. It was so hard to realize they wore exposure proof clothing and double rubber gloves so they couldn't get this nasty stuff on them, and that is what they were injecting into my veins. This was so scary to me. This treatment took about two hours. After the chemo, they flushed again for a few minutes to be sure the tubes were empty, and veins were flushed.

Now it was time to head for home, I was feeling a little tired, so Mari drove and I rested. We did make one stop, before we left Hays and that was at the Quick Shop to get a snowball, which was a frozen soda, and my treat for having treatment. When we got to WaKeeney, I had to make a stop at Gibson's to get three new prescriptions, one to take right after treatment, one if I felt a little nauseous, the third if I felt really sick or wanted to fall asleep, as this pill had a tendency to make a person drowsy, and a refill on my pain patches.

We made it home and had a bite to eat and read my mail. I got a letter from the local cancer society, which was a surprise. I didn't even know there was a group that helped local people through their trials. They sent me a paper to fill out so they could give me a gas credit card which I could use for my trips to Hays to treatment. There was also information about a program at the hospital called "Wellness." It is a program just for cancer patients to help keep up their strength and help them to get through this difficult time. The program was on Tuesdays and Thursdays from eight until noon, and free to cancer patients. The nurse in charge was Christie, and she was trained in cancer wellness. I gave her a call and told her I was interested and asked a few questions about the program. She took our blood pressure and monitored our activities to help us to gain our strength and balance back. She explained many of the things that we would be doing. This program wasn't just for the physical side of cancer, it was also for our mental side, as only cancer patients are allowed to be with us on those days so we can talk and give each other support. I thought that sounded good and wanted to participate, she said great but I can't do the physical part of the program while I am getting treatment because we can't exercise for twenty-four hours after chemo, but I was welcome to come, meet and visit with the people in the program. I thanked her and said I would come when I could and meet everyone.

What a crazy day, I was sure I would sleep, at least I hoped I would. The first day of treatment wasn't so bad. I hope I get along as well for the rest of them, but I'm thinking it will get harder and harder. Day two here I come. My appointment was set for 11:00 each day except for the days I see the doctor, then it was 10:30 every Monday. Tuesday, Mari and I headed out for Hays to get day number two started. We arrived at the cancer center and it was the same as it was the day before, first the radiation side, then the chemo side. This time the chemo treatment was the same procedure, except the treatment itself took four hours. That really seemed like a long time, and since it was lunch time, I could order lunch from the hospital if I felt like eating. Food right then did not even sound good, I was afraid chemo was starting to make me feel a little sick to my stomach. I told my nurse and she gave me something for the nausea, in a few minutes it made me feel better. Finally, it was time for us to return home, by the time we got there is was almost supper time. Glad Mari was there to cook so I didn't have to, I felt really tired and needed a nap, so a nap it was.

I was starting to depend on the Fentanyl patches; I found it hard to wait until it was time for a new one. I asked for Mari to change to a new one, but she made me wait. If it wasn't for Mari, I would really be in trouble, she would watch and not put a new one on until it was time. That told me I was getting addicted—so no more. When the last one came off, that was the last one, I'll just have to accept the pain and deal with it. Surely after a few treatments the tumor will shrink and the coughing and pain will let up.

Day three, as it turns out, was the worst of the week. Radiation was the same, but the chemo was a five-hour treatment, and that was way too long to stay awake, so I found myself dozing off for a couple of hours. I did remember to take my nausea pill before we came so I didn't feel too bad, it just made me so sleepy. Everyone at the cancer center was so nice and caring, they always made sure we were comfortable, if we need a warm blanket, something to drink or eat. We were more than just a number to them; we were sick, and they are there for us.

Mari asked me what sounded good for supper, and the only thing I could think that even remotely sounded good was watermelon. It may have been a little early for them to be particularly good. Mari left me for a few minutes so she could stop by the grocery store and pick up a watermelon. It wasn't too bad for being early in the year. I could eat a little, the smell of something cooking really turned my stomach.

Day four, I felt really tired that morning, I guess that long chemo day really hit me heard. What a way to spend my birthday. I took my shower and had to rest before I could dress, and after I dressed, I went into the living room and had to sit in my chair and take a nap. Wow, I was surprised how hard it hit me this time. Mari always had coffee when she got up and the smell of it really turned my stomach, and I always liked coffee. She would always make me eat something to start my day even if I didn't want to, but I guess that is one of the reasons why she was there. Time to go came way too soon, and this was only the first week. I don't know what to expect, but surely it can't be another five-hour treatment, that was the tough one.

We arrived at the center again and things were the same, radiation then chemo. Chemo was a four-hour treatment so that wasn't so bad, but I still took a nap, my energy got less with each treatment, and I found myself wanting to sleep more, but I haven't lost my hair, maybe I won't. On our way home I thought, *Four down and only one more to go—this week. I couldn't even stay awake until we got home, I dozed off shortly after we hit the interstate. Wow, fifteen minutes in the car and I'm asleep, but maybe that was good for me, or I wouldn't do it, right?* That was what I told myself anyway, most of the time when I slept during the day, my mind was not wondering and that was good, because I did not always sleep very well at night.

Supper. I did not want to eat, but Mari encouraged me to eat a little bit. She said I have to keep up my strength, and she was right, but I was really feeling nauseous, so I took a pill I am to take after treatment if I feel that way. My supper comes up anyway, and I hate vomiting more than anything, I'd rather have diarrhea for a week then to vomit once. With that being said, I took my third pill for the nausea, and it worked but it also made be sleepy. I slept all night and that made me feel better the next morning.

Yea! It was Friday and last day of treatment that week. When we arrived, the radiation department called me back and the first thing they did was take my blood. This was how it was each week, so the doctors could see how my body tolerated the treatments. I then proceeded to my radiation treatment, which was the same as it had been all week. Chemo treatment was another four-hour session, so I guessed that was the way it would be from there on out, Monday--two hours, Tuesday, Thursday and Friday--four hours and Wednesday would be the grueling five-hour treatment. What a way to spend my days each week for six weeks, an eighty-mile round trip for treatments. I guessed if it worked and got rid of my cancer, I could make this schedule work. I was sure looking forward to the weekend and no long trip or treatments, so I could get some energy and hopefully some strength back.

Saturday was a day of rest, I didn't do much of anything and that wasn't such a bad idea, rest was what I needed. Sunday was a good day, I woke up, showered, and dressed for church, and looked forward to eating out after Mass. It was Easter Sunday, and Jeremy asked us to have dinner at his house. He had invited both of his brothers and families. Jason and his family came, but Joshua's family couldn't come. Allison was so cute making sure Grandma had what she needed, whether it was a place to sit, or a blanket when I took my nap. We had a nice meal, I couldn't eat too much, but it was delicious, and what I did eat stayed down, which was good. Thank you, Lord, for giving me this day, I really needed it with my family, and hopefully I can make another week of treatment without much trouble.

Monday morning came around way too fast, and so did the time to leave for Hays, but here we go again. I at least I kind of knew what to expect. The first thing was a doctor visit to see how she thinks the treatments were going and how my body was tolerating the treatment. My blood tests were pretty good. The only thing I needed to watch was my protein intake, as my hemoglobin is getting low, I needed to keep it up to at least ten or they would have to give me blood before continuing. That might be hard to do, I really did not have much of an appetite, so we may need to find some protein supplement that doesn't taste so bad.

With the doctor visit over, it was time for radiation and chemo treatments. Monday was the short day so it was not too bad. It still bothered me that the nurses put on so much protection and they were putting that awful stuff in my blood stream. Mari went to the store to check out the protein options while I was in treatment, and she found a couple protein supplements for me to try. We decided to stop and get something for lunch to see if I could eat. Mexican food sounded kind of good, so we gave it a try. It tasted fine, and I ate it all, which was good for me. We stopped by the Quick Shop to get snowballs, after all, it was our regular stop before heading home.

Nap time seemed to be a regular activity for me those days, but I had my pinochle card club that night at my sister-in-law Carol's house. Mari will be the substitute for us. We had supper and headed out for a nice evening of cards with the girls. The time ticked away, and we talked about how I was doing before we left for the evening. Someone said, "Gee you haven't even lost your hair." I put my fingers in my hair and guess what--I pulled out a whole handful of hair, so I guess it was starting to fall out. Darn—I was hoping that I would not lose my hair. I did notice that there was no root on the hair in my hand, so it broke off at the scalp.

Treatment for the rest of the week was about the same as it was the previous week. Our trials for this week were at home time. We were trying the protein supplement to help with my hemoglobin. The first one was awful and it made me feel nauseous, so that one was not going to work. We even tried to put it in an ice cream malt, and that didn't help. The next one we tried was called Pure Protein and it really didn't taste too bad. We used it for the milk in the malt and it tasted pretty good, so that was the one I was able to use. Mari was good about trying different foods to try to get me to eat, but nothing really tasted very good, my appetite just wasn't there. I was starting to lose weight and the Oncologist really did not want me to lose, but I just couldn't eat.

Mari's daughter from Kansas City called, and asked if Mari could come stay with the grand children while she was at a work-related meeting. Of course she had to go help out. I was sure I could get help to take me to treatment, or David could take me. She would leave on the coming weekend, so I had the weekend to find help. Treatment went pretty well that week until Thursday. When I woke for the day, I could not see out of my right eye and wondered what the heck was going on. When I got the cancer center, I asked to see my doctor's assistant while I was receiving treatment. She came to see me and asked what the problem was? I told her that I could not see. She did some checking and they decided the treatment had caused a part of my retina to tear away and caused a flag-like affect that obstructed the light from getting to my retina, so I was unable to see. She set up an appointment at the Retinol Center in Wichita for confirmation and to see what could be done. This was a rare condition, but it does happen, wouldn't you know, it would happen to me. Not being able to see out of my right eye messes up depth perception, so I was unable to drive, which made finding drivers for the next couple of weeks even more important. Friday was quite uneventful, blood work, radiation, chemo, home, and naptime.

Yea!! Another weekend arrived, time to recharge and catch my breath. Saturday morning I started looking for drivers by looking through the many cards that had been sent to me, to see which friends said, "if there was anything they could do to help." I had one friend, Linda, who brought us food every Thursday afternoon, so I really didn't want to ask her for any more help. I'm sure I have other friends that didn't have regular jobs, who would be willing to help out. It was heartwarming to go back through the cards and read them again. I have great friends. I only had to make four calls to fill drivers for the eleven treatment days, no one I asked turned me down. Someone asked me how my boys were doing with all that was going on. I said they check in with me about every day. They asked what I told them, did I just say I was doing okay? No, I said I tell them the truth.

Sunday morning, I woke up early and decided I was still among the living, so we decided to go to church. That felt good, even though I had to stay a distance from the congregation because of my depressed immune system and sit in the choir loft, it was still great hearing God's word. When Mass was over, there were quite a few people waiting for me to come out to see how I was doing. We stood and talked for a few minutes, then a couple friends asked us to have dinner with them at the Pizza Hut. My desire to eat good food was greater than my need for so much food, I just couldn't eat very much, but I gave it a try. We decided to stay in town and play cards with some friends, which was a lot of fun and good to do something normal for a change.

Deep breath, it was Monday. My hair was falling out by the hands full, I took a shower and the drain was totally full with hair. Now what do I do, let it fall out and plug the drain or have someone shave it off? Something to think about this week, decision, decision, what will I look like bald? Janeen was taking me Monday, Tuesday and Wednesday, and she was aware that I must be at the cancer center early for my doctor's appointment to see how my blood work looked.

Dr. O'Dea came in looking pretty as usual, I don't understand the high heels though--on her feet all day and wears those crazy things. The blood looked a bit like I was having toleration issues, hemoglobin was still getting lower, potassium was too low, and sodium was also too low. She ordered a unit of blood for tomorrow before treatment, followed by the chemo, it would take about an hour longer than usual. Doctor said I needed to drink Gatorade, at least one bottle a day, and all the water I want. I needed to have one meal with chicken bouillon for the sodium shortage, either as a drink or add noodles to make a kind of soup. Those instructions really did not make my day, I really do not like Gatorade or chicken bouillon, the noodles and cream of chicken or mushroom soup would make it tolerable, hopefully.

While I was waiting for chemo, a person who checked on the welfare of patients sat and talked to me for a bit. She said when I wanted to go into the wig shop, I was welcome to take any of the wigs and hats I wanted as long as I needed them. Janeen told me she would be more than glad to help me pick a wig out for when I needed it. We did go out and share a lunch, and of course I had to stop and get my snowball before heading home. On the way home she asked if I would mind seeing what the radiation treatment was all about, and I told her that I didn't think the girls would mind if she went back with me.

The next morning, I asked Mellissa if Janeen could see how the radiation treatment worked. She was more than glad to take her back into the room where the nurses were and explained everything to her, how precise the machine was and how it all worked. Janeen was so appreciative of the explanation and the chance to see how it all worked. In between treatments we went into the wig shop and she helped me pick out a wig. It was amazing how natural it looked and how well it matched my greying hair, even the cut was the same as I wore my hair. That was the day I had a unit of blood, then chemo. All went well, only tired and a little sick, but this too would pass.

Tuesday evening a couple of friends came out to play cards, which was fun. It was close to 11:00, and when they were getting ready to leave I asked if they someone would be willing to shave my head. Bernita said she was too scared to do it, but Pat said she would do it for me. I got the clippers and cape, put a short guard on the clippers and handed it to Pat, and sat on the chair. She started at the nape of my neck and headed up. The cut was not a shave but almost, but at least I wouldn't plug the drain anymore or shed like a dog. I never really liked to wear hats, but I would have to get used to it unless I just wanted to go out bare headed or wear my new wig. The weather was getting warmer and the wig was hot, so the hat it was.

Treatment for rest of the week was pretty uneventful. The stress that week was the things I had to do at home, drink Gatorade and make myself eat a bowl of chicken bouillon to which I did add noodles and cream soup to make a chicken noodle soup. Since Mari wasn't here, I had to do most of the cooking, as David isn't much of a cook, he would make breakfast of scrambled eggs and toast which was pretty tasty, and at least I would eat a little.

Saturday. David decided he could take me to town to purchase some groceries, which was the first time I wore a hat over my bald head in public. One does not feel out of place at the cancer center because we all are in the same boat. I walked into the grocery store and people stared at me then looked away, so they wouldn't have to look at me. I tell you that really made me feel strange and invisible. How come a man can shave his head and no one seems to care, but a woman, even wearing a hat makes everyone seem so uncomfortable. I was still the same person, I just didn't have any hair.

People who know me and what I was going through would stop and speak to me, and ask how I was doing, that made me feel good. Most acquaintances would give me a hug and ask how I was feeling. Friends are so important in my life, I don't know how people get along without anyone knowing that you have cancer, and not having a support group of people around them. With this being my first time out in public, there were a lot of questions and discussions in the isles of the grocery store. That probably was one of the longest times it took me to buy only a few groceries, but it was good to know so many people cared. We were only in town for a couple hours, and I almost fell asleep just driving the eight miles home. After the groceries were put away it soon became nap time.

Sunday. I am glad that mass isn't until 10:30 so I didn't have to get up too early to be able to go. Sitting upstairs in the choir loft to be a little distanced from the congregation was a good place to go, but the climb up the stairs was a killer, steps really took it out of me. I am glad that I was able to go to church so I could thank God for getting me through the first half of my treatments and pray that He would get me through the next three weeks. I wore my wig, and no one even noticed that it wasn't my real hair, so I really didn't get too many stares. After church we went out to eat with friends again and afterward, we played cards. I really needed friendship to keep me going.

Sunday evening, I had a surprise, my sister JoAnn came in for a visit and to help me. We were sitting at the table talking and she said, "Gee it is good that you have not lost your hair." I just smiled and put my hand on my hair and lifted off my wig, and said, "Really." Her eyes got as big as saucers and we started to laugh. She said she could not tell it was not my hair, it looked so natural and the cut and color even looked the same.

Chapter Four

SECOND HALF OF TREATMENT

Don't put off until tomorrow what you should do today.

Three weeks went by in my treatment, and I was feeling like a stranger in my own skin. People found it hard to look at me, they looked away instead of just saying hello. The man I love lay beside me every night and he found it hard to give me a hug. I ask why and he said, "I don't want to hurt you." I wish he understood that not hugging me hurt more. I didn't understand why people thought I had leprosy instead of cancer. Just because I looked a little pale, wore a hat because I had no hair—I was still the same person I was before I was diagnosed with this disease. Do they look away because they don't know what to say, or maybe just because I have no hair? I don't think I smelled bad, I wore pull over shirts so I know my buttons weren't open—I just wanted to yell out, "I'm still me!"

Monday of week four, as always, started with the doctor appointment. My blood work looked better, my hemoglobin was up a little, so no blood needed to be given, my sodium and potassium were pretty good, but she wanted me to continue with the Gatorade and bouillon, and continue to eat protein and the supplement I was taking. Even though I lost thirty pounds, she still felt I was doing fine with the treatment regimen, and there was no need to change. She wanted to make sure I was sleeping and if I needed something to help, she would give me a prescription. I told her that the nausea medicine took care of the times I was not able to sleep. I was to continue to use it, sleep was very necessary for the healing process.

During chemo, one of the girls asked what I did for pastime. I told her I made jewelry. I had some pictures on my phone that I shared and she asked if I would bring some and share it with the girls. I said heck no, I would love to bring it, so I made up a display to take with me the next day.

Tuesday morning after my shower I happened to notice that the little stubble of hair that Pat had left on my head was gone. I was bald as a turkey egg, but it sure was easy to wash, and I didn't have to fix my hair. I think the warm shower water really made it hard for me to breathe. I just never took a breath without thinking about it, just didn't take breathing for granted anymore. I think the warm water was part of the reason that after showering I needed to rest a bit before and while I dressed. After a protein malt for breakfast, it was about time for the trip to Hays again, I had put my jewelry display on the porch so I wouldn't forget to take it.

I started with radiation again as usual, but that day was a bit different. I was taking off my shirt and bra when I heard a voice say, "Well, hello Anita, how are you and Mr. Schneider doing?" It was Garret, a young man from WaKeeney, the person who did the radiation treatment on me. I had seen him a few times in the waiting room, so I knew that he worked there, but never had I visited with him in the radiation room. As I came out from behind the screen with a hand towel over my breasts, I felt a little embarrassed, but I don't know why, he has seen me during treatment lying on the table for weeks now. We visited for a bit about things and then it was time to get radiation started. I have known Garret for a long time, he was one of the boys David taught in school. After my radiation, I stopped at the little baskets of Aquaphor and picked up a few tubes. The spot on my back from the radiation burns really hurt and hopefully that would help them heal.

I was called back to the chemo treatment area. Sara noticed I was carrying my necklace display board, and she was excited to see what I had. As she was getting me ready, a couple of the other girls came to see what I had to show. After they looked at my jewelry, I sold five pieces to them, and had an order for a couple more custom-made pieces. I was so happy. JoAnn was so happy that I sold some pieces. Selling those pieces and having the girls think they were really pretty and well made, made me feel good and made my chemo treatment a little less hard, at least for one day.

The chemo came up from the lab, so it was time for me get my treatment. I had no clue JoAnn had never seen anyone get a treatment. When Sara got herself ready for the treatment by putting on a water proof garment, double rubber gloves and started to run the chemo, JoAnn's eyes got big, her mouth dropped open and she could not believe that they were putting that chemo into my body. Reality hit her like a baseball bat, I just told her that was the way it was done through my port, and she just realized what was happening to me.

The rest of the week was pretty much uneventful, just same oh, same oh, an eighty-mile round trip to treatments and naps. The more treatments that I had the more I was affected, I was more tired and ate less and slept more. Sometimes it was even hard for me to remember what was going on, where I had been and what time of the day it was. I just hoped that all that nasty chemo stuff was working, but there was no way to tell until after my treatments were finished. I had one week to go and then about three months later I would have a CT scan to see how it worked. One more week of treatment to go, and I will have Mari back to care for me, which always made me feel more comfortable.

Yea!! It was Saturday, a day to rejuvenate and get ready for the next and last week of treatment forever, I hope. One would think that you would get used to looking in the mirror and seeing that bald head and sad eyes after seeing them for weeks, but I'm not sure I ever got used to that face looking back at me. I just kept telling myself that it would all be worth it when it was over, and the tumor turned into a ball of scar tissue, and the cancer was under control. I did not think I would ever get used to the way people looked away, not able to look me in the eyes, it made me feel invisible, I didn't get it, I was still me.

The chemo fog was starting to affect my memory, sometimes it was hard for me to recall a name or even just a word I wanted to use. For instance, one day I wanted a thing that you put dirt in, and add a flower, you know the little thing that it goes in. David looked at me and said, "You want a pot," and he stated to laugh. I started to cry because he had laughed. He just did not understand that the word "pot" just wouldn't come out. Some people call it chemo fog, I call it chemo brain. It is almost like a stroke patient, when I tried to think of a word--it just would not come. It really made me feel frustrated and the harder I tried, the harder it was to come to me. I hoped this passed and I won't be this way forever.

Week six, last week, final week of treatments, I'd almost made it through this growling time of duel treatments, radiation and chemo. Now my thoughts wondered, *What next, will this be all the treatment I will ever have, is the cancer gone, has the radiation killed the tumors, has the chemo killed all the little cancer seeds, what will my hair look like when it grows back, if it grows back, will my appetite come back, will food continue to taste bad, will my energy come back, will I ever be "normal" again?*

I did not need to think about these things it was only Sunday, I had another day to rejuvenate, go to church and pray that I would make it through. The people of our parish are so nice and caring, they always stopped and chat and find out how things were going and send prayers and love. Lunch and cards with friends were always a good way to spend a Sunday. I seemed to run out of gas, but I didn't want to go home so I pushed myself for as long as I could. But eventually the tiredness won and off to home we went. JoAnn had to leave, and it was hard to see her go. It was a nice visit and so much help to me.

Mari made it back on Sunday evening, she seemed to have a good time caring for her grand kids, and I'm sure the break from my crazy routine was a welcome change. Mari was quite surprised how thin and pale I had gotten in the past two weeks. She just said, "So you had no one to make you eat, huh?" I said, "I guess not, but I did miss you anyway." I had lost fifty-five pounds by that time, so I guess she could tell.

I told Mari about writing a letter to the editor of our local paper and she thought it was a good idea. I called the editor, who just happens to be a friend of mine.

WESTERN KANSAS WORLD
May 14, 2015
Only in a Small Town

It seemed like the word about me having cancer got around town before I even got it confirmed. But you know that is OK because as soon as people knew, the words of encouragement and prayers started coming to me, only in a small town. After the initial diagnosis, came a series of tests to determine the type of cancer and the extent of the spread of the cancer cells. Even though the diagnosis was cancer, it was contained in the left lobe of my lung, very involved with key functions making it inoperable. I had to undergo a major chest surgery to get the biopsy of what kind and how it was to be treated. Word of this got around quickly also and the get-well cards and gifts arrived at the hospital, only in a small town.

Chemotherapy and radiation started about three weeks later and cards of encouragement, prayers and well wishes seemed to come in daily as well as

31

phone calls, only in a small town. David was there for me every step of the way, and I felt he needed to do what he needed to do to keep some type of normality in his world because I seemed to turn in upside down. My sister Mari came to be a member of my in-house support team, driving me to chemo and radiation on a daily basis making sure I ate and drank. I had offers from friends to drive me or do whatever I needed only in a small town.

A week after my first round of chemo was over, my sister needed to go back to Gardner and stay with her grandchildren, a tough job but someone had to do it. So, with her departure I needed drivers to take me to my daily treatments. I made some phone calls to the friends that had volunteered to help and within a short time I had all eleven slots filled, only in a small town.

The worst symptoms I had was being tired, taking at least two naps a day, and having no energy. Having something to eat did not seem to be a problem as we have many friends that bring us food and it always seems to be enough for multiple meals, only in a small town.

A week after my first round a chemo came the hair loss. Losing large amounts quickly, I decided to have a couple of friends shave it off for me one night after playing cards, only in a small town.

Feeling pretty well on the Thursday night of the Read Theater at the Studio, I called a friend to take me along with her and I was really glad I did. It was a fun evening despite my tiredness, I had a good time. With many friends attending I also received many hugs and continued prayers. Before we left that evening there was even a group prayer, only in a small town.

I have completed my second round of chemotherapy and am on my last days of radiation. My sister came

32

back to help me through it again, but the words of encouragement and prayers are still coming in, only in a small town.

I cannot tell you how much this means to me; the accuracy and quickness of Lisa Frost, my family, friends, prayers, food, cards, phone calls and the love that is shown, <u>only in a small town</u>.

Anita Schneider

Last week of treatment here I come—Monday was very uneventful, radiation and chemo were the same. Mari was back so we definitely had to stop for snowballs, since she had not had one for two whole weeks, but that was okay because I really wanted one too. On the way home I fell asleep in the car, but I guess Mari and I stayed up too late talking on how the last couple of weeks went.

Tuesday however, was a bit different, I woke up, showered, dressed, ate a bit, and then it was nap time as usual. I woke up and asked Mari if it was time to go to Hays, and she laughed and said that we had already been there. I cannot believe I did not remember the whole morning, any of it, the trip, treatments and home again. We had even stopped for a snowball and since I was not totally with it, Mari just put mine in the refrigerator. I guess I will just have it for my afternoon snack, and of course Mari made me eat some protein with it. Yep, she was back and taking charge as usual.

Wednesday was a bit better, as far as remembering the trip and treatments, but I did not feel very well all the way home and when we arrived home I lost my cookies, so they say. It was a tough rest of the day, even my vomiting pills didn't help much that afternoon, I was glad that I finally fell asleep later that evening and slept until morning. Thank God for those uninterrupted, restful nights. I would wake and feel so refreshed.

Since this was my last week I decided to have Mari make each of the departments a special treat. We took the radiation department a jelly roll and the chemo department a bunt cake. They really thought it was nice of us to bring them something special, but everyone was just wonderful in the way I was treated. It was the least that we could.

Then it was time to wait, I had to wait six weeks before I could have a CT to see how the treatment worked. Waiting was so hard, having alone time left me with my thoughts, and my mind had the bad habit of always thinking the worst.

The group of people who worked in the radiation department gave me a bookmark and I want to share it, I keep it on my refrigerator and read it often.

WHAT CANCER CANNOT DO—*Cancer is so limited...*
It cannot cripple Love—It cannot shatter Hope—It cannot corrode Faith—It cannot destroy Peace—It cannot kill Friendship—It cannot suppress Memories—It cannot silence Courage—It cannot invade the Soul—It cannot steal eternal Life—It cannot conquer the Spirit.

Time to think about the last five months; terrible cough, x-ray, cancer diagnosis, pulmonologist unsuccessful biopsy, cardiovascular biopsy, confirmation of Adenocarcinoma lung cancer, CT scan, MRI, PET scan, radiation and chemo treatments, blood infusion, weight loss, no appetite, total body hair loss, loss of energy, frequent vomiting are the physical side effects of my cancer. The cancer treatment made my head perspire profusely during the night and it had such an awful smell that I actually ruined two pillows. I guess it was the chemo leaving my body. I tried to wash them but the horrible smell remained.

Telling my family that I had cancer was one of the hardest things, and I always told them the truth as to how I was feeling or how things were going. I always taught my boys that lying is never an option, always tell the truth and deal with the consequences afterward. The wondering what will happen next, the unknown was so scary, the sleepless nights, the sadness in people's eyes, the way some people avoided eye contact, some of them talked louder to me--I'm not having hearing problems, and the constant mind wondering are many of the mental side effects of my cancer. I have learned who my real friends are, the many, many cards, calls, visits, food, card playing and the prayers are some of the good things I noticed since my diagnosis.

Now that school was out for the summer I got to see Allison more, she would come along with her dad to see me. One day, she and a couple of her friends came, and I didn't know they were coming so I did not have my wig on. When the kids came, I told them I had a bad disease and it made all my hair fall out. The young boy with her just said that his dad was bald so what's the difference, a man's bald head or a woman's bald head, it was okay. Out of the mouths of babes. We had a nice visit and it was good to spend time with Allison and friends.

My sister, Irene's sixty-fifth birthday was that month and she decided to have all her sisters come to California for her birthday celebration. I really did not have much energy but I didn't want to miss it either, so I decided to go. I told the girls that they would have to take it easy with me and give me time to rest, and I hoped I would be fine. Before it was time to go, I decided I needed to get my nails done, so I called and Liz had an appointment the next day. After she finished I asked how much and she said that it has been taken care of, I asked by whom. She didn't want to tell me but finally did, she said Bernita had paid for it. Bernita just knew what I needed. After I left, I had to stop by the drug store and thank her. Having my nails done made me feel so much better. I was ready to go, I packed my clothes, a couple of hats and my wig and off we went to California. In-between my naps we had a great time and everyone was so kind to me, it made me feel like myself again.

By the time we got back and I had some rest, it was time for my CT and then a week later to see my Oncologist so we could tell how the treatment worked. Mari went back to Gardner, so David and I were on our own and he would have to take me

35

to appointments again. He really didn't mind and was really interested on how things had come along also.

I had been feeling pretty well and hopeful that things were going to be good. The day finally came to see the Doctor, I was called back, weighed, blood pressure taken and waiting for Dr. O'Dea. When she came in with my reports in her hands she had a smile, so I thought that things were good. She told us the CT looked pretty good but (Oh no, not a "but," that is never good) she thought another three weeks of treatment were warranted, with double the dose of chemo without the radiation.

Tears filled my eyes and she explained that it is for assurance, we really didn't want things to start back up again. I knew she knew what she was talking about, it was just hard to hear that I had to have more chemo. I was so hoping the cancer was gone, and I could have my port removed and be normal again. I guess that was not meant to be and I would have to continue treatment. Double the dose, how could I handle that, no radiation but double chemo? I guess if I have to, I have to. Before we left that day, my appointment was set for the following Monday to start treatment again.

Seven weeks had passed since my last treatment and my hair was starting to come in. Mari called me her Chia pet, then Spike as it continued to grow. With this new double dose chemo I bet my hair would come out again, the last time I lost all body hair except my eye brows. My first treatment was quite uneventful, I did not feel any different than I did with the first dosage. So David wouldn't have to take me every day, I called on friends again, and I had no problem getting them to take me. They seemed more than happy to do it. I had treatments on the first four days of the week. On Friday I had to go to the outpatient clinic at our hometown hospital and get a Neulasta shot, which was a shot to help my body ward off infection since my chemo was so strong. The side effects of the shot was muscle pain, believe me it had a horrible reaction. I had lightning bolts in every muscle in my body, it was awful, it made me shirk with pain with every beat of my heart, and it lasted for about thirty-six hours.

I was going into my second week of treatment when I received a letter from Dr. O'Dea. She said she was taking a position in Kansas City with the Breast Cancer Center and that Dr. Rodrigues would take over my care. I was a little apprehensive getting a new Oncologist so late in my treatment, I just hoped he was good and I liked him.

I went to the bank on Monday and was talking to a friend, Mary Jo, who is a cancer survivor. I happened to mention my reaction to the Neulasta shot and she told me she had the same reaction and was told to take a Clairton the day before, one the day of, and one the day after, to see it that helped. She said it really helped her. I hoped that it would help because the lightning bolts were horrible. My friend Mickie was taking me to treatments that week and while I was getting treatment she would walk on the trail located next the hospital. It is a really nice trail, I just wished I had enough energy to walk it too.

I had a new reaction that day. I had hand pain in the nerves shooting up my arm, numb feet and shooting pains up my legs also. If my feet aren't numb, they hurt like walking on a bed of tacks. I wasn't not sure what was going on, but I bet I would find out from Dr. Rodriguez at my next appointment. The rest of the week's treatments went fine, just tired.

I don't think I got as sick as I did when I had radiation and chemo at the same time. The radiation made me really tired, and the chemo made me sick, and when you put them together it was quite uncomfortable. Friday came and it was Neulasta time. I took Clairton on Thursday, one on Friday morning and I took the last one on Saturday, and sure hoped it helped. After my shot, I did not get a reaction so I guessed it was going to help—YEA!!

This was my last week of chemo and my first appointment with my new Oncologist, Dr. Rodriguez. I looked forward to both. David and I headed to Hays for my appointment, they called my back, weight, blood pressure and ready for the Doctor to come in. Dr. Rodriguez was a very nice looking young doctor with a wonderful personality. He seemed to be kind, caring and wanted his patients to be comfortable with him and what was going on in their lives. I asked him about the pains that I was having in my hands and feet. He said it was neuropathy, and it is a bad pain that is not very controllable. He said there were some medicines we could try such as Lyrica; he gave me a script for it to try. He thought I was doing really good with treatment and wanted me to have the last week of treatment. We would have a CT in three months to check the progress. I would have to have my port flushed every month, either in WaKeeney or come to the cancer center, to be sure it stays active and clean. After my doctor's appointment I had chemo and took my nap while the infusion was running.

The last week was pretty uneventful, but I prepared for my Neulasta shot so I wouldn't have reactions again. Last treatment, last shot forever I hoped. The pretreatment worked, and I didn't have any reactions, those were my thoughts for the day.

Chapter Five

WAITING FOR RESULTS

Dealing with problems and concerns early in the day.

It was the first time since January that I had not been poked, prodded, tested, had biopsies, implanted, radiation, and chemotherapy or treatment of any kind. I felt relieved, but still a little scared as to what was happening inside. *Were the tumors gone, was there anything else growing or have I had my last treatments? I just didn't know what to expect. What would the future bring, was my cancer gone, and would I be able to have my port removed?* Three months to think about these things, I hoped I could leave it alone and not dwell on things for the entire time. But I was sure that as the time got closer, I would worry more about it.

I received a phone call from the *Hays Daily News*, the biggest newspaper for about one hundred miles. She wanted to print a special article on my small business "Nita's Notions." A friend of mine had told her about me, and she thought it would be a nice advertisement for my business. I told her I would be more than happy to give her an interview, I just needed a little heads up to get my wig on. She said she would give me a call the following week when they were leaving Hays and that would give me plenty of time to get ready.

Nor'wester

August 23, 2015

BUSY HANDS

WaKeeney—It started as a simple family fun activity for WaKeeney resident Anita Schneider. But before she knew it, desire and dedication sprang from the craft she never knew she'd like.

Like many families, Schneider and her three sisters make an effort to get together every so often for bonding time and during this time, they typically work on fun projects or crafts.

"My sisters are the reason I got into this," Schneider said. "My sister in California, Irene, usually brings some kind of craft idea."

A few years ago, a jewelry project was thrown into the mix, and typically viewing herself as a perfectionist, Schneider wondered if she should even bother trying.

"I thought there was no way I could do it," she said. "I just always want things to be perfect, so I figured I would never get it right."

It was only after she learned the technique of wrapping rocks that she began to feel herself become intrigued by the process.

"I kind of liked wrapping rocks, and that's how this all started," Schneider said.

It didn't take long for Schneider to start creating a variety of unique jewelry including necklaces, earrings, bracelets and rings.

She collaborated different stones, beads, wire and tools to begin her journey of potentially turning a hobby into a business.

"They are all natural stones and glass beads. I'm not real crazy about the synthetic ones," she said. "I like to use the real stuff."

Her unique styles obviously caught the eyes of many, who quickly began inquiring about the jewelry.

"I had people come up to me and want to know where I got my necklace," she said. "Then I just sold it to them right off my neck."

Selling her designs as she was wearing them was not a rarity, and similar circumstances began to occur more frequently.

"I've sold them at department stores, airports, grocery stores—right off my neck," she said. "That is kind of what pushed me to take it a little more seriously."

Schneider began making more and more jewelry and started selling her products at crafts fairs and other locations under her jewelry-making business, Nita's Notions.

She stayed busy creating pieces for repeat customers conducting private parties and even selling her products in different local businesses including Gibson Health Mart and the Studio.

"I find her work unique because she is the only artist I have that makes jewelry with twisted metal, beads and with rocks," said Lynelle

Shubert, owner of the Studio. *"I've even had customers bring in things for her to wrap in wire for them."*

"The jewelry has a very earthy feeling that people like and the pieces are always one-of-a-kind."

Schneider's husband, David, supports her craft and has constructed a desk at home for her workspace and display boards to hang the products on. He even bought her a trailer for her birthday so she could transport items to craft fairs more easily.

"Once I started selling them at craft fairs, I did fairly well," she said. "I make enough money to keep it going."

Though her ambition was strong and steady, the jewelry-maker was shaken by news she received in February that ultimately would slow her pace.

She said. "I was diagnosed with lung cancer," she said. "I haven't made as much jewelry as I did in the past because it's hard for me to see now and strength is a real problem for me."

After biopsy surgery, numerous CAT scans and MRIs, chemotherapy and radiation began in April.

Schneider said the chemotherapy weakened her eyes, and because of that, she continues to work on pieces mostly by feel.

"When you're dealt a bad hand, you're dealt a bad hand," she said.

But the jewelry-making helped in more ways than she ever could have expected.

"It is good for me because it keeps my mind distracted and my hands busy," she said. "I just keep trying to fill my boards while I hope for a good report from the doctor so I can keep it going."

Schneider continues her work averaging three to four house a day creating unique, one-of-a-kind pieces of jewelry.

"People like it, and the reaction I get from them makes me just want to keep doing more," she said. "I want everyone to like what I make them, and I plan to keep doing this as long as I have opportunities before me.

For more information about Nita's Notions or to inquire about a purchase, call (785) 743-2668 or email Anita at schneid2@ruraltel.net.

This newspaper article was really good for me, it made me feel good about what I was doing and brought me some new customers. The lady who did the interview said if she didn't know I was wearing a wig, she never would have known it. My oldest brother and his wife came to see me, and they didn't know it was a wig either.

I was even surprised that they came, they were always telling me that I was supposed to go to a bigger hospital, because they knew what they were doing. That is not what a cancer patient wanted to hear, we wanted support, not people telling us our choices were wrong. I made my choice for different reasons, and I was pleased with the treatment I received. The people at the cancer center where I went were awesome, made me feel important, and that they really cared for me and about me.

A couple of weeks later, Mickie and Elaine decided they were going to take me away for a few days. I agreed to go and needed to get away from my thoughts and share some time away. We headed off on a huge bus to Branson, Missouri, for a few days. It was an all-inclusive trip, the bus ride, hotel rooms, meals, shows, and someone who knew where to go and what to do. We went to a few shows and they were awesome, the food was good, the company was good, and the time away was really needed. There was only one experience that I really didn't need. We were on the bus and I was feeling a little warm and dizzy, so I took off my hat and my totally bald head was just there. A lady a few seats behind me kept looking at me and whispering to her companion. I just wanted to yell at her and tell her that I have cancer and the treatment made my hair fall out, so stop staring and get over it—I'm still a person, and I don't need your whispers. But I didn't.

On the trip home we stopped at a little cheese shop, and the cheese was unreal, they even had cheese that tasted like chocolate, but the texture was still like cheese—really weird. They had a lot of gift items, and a lot of tasting opportunities, trying to sell their products. Of course it worked, I think we all purchased something. Our little get-away was a lot of fun and a much needed breath of fresh thoughts. That funny feeling I had in the bus didn't go away that day. On our way home in Elaine's car, I lost my lunch, but fortunately she had a plastic bag in her car and I got it in time, so I didn't make a smelly mess. I'm not sure why that happened but it did, and I slept all that evening and night at home.

Since I wasn't having chemo, I decided to start going to the Wellness exercise program at the hospital. I went in to talk to Christie to find out when and what I needed to do to come into the group. We were to meet on Tuesdays and Thursdays between 8:00 a.m. and noon. Most of the girls came in about 9:00 to do their workouts, so I decided I would come at the same time, so we could be support for each other. I knew all the girls who came so it made it easy for me to fit in, and I felt at ease talking to them.

A month went by so quickly, and I had to have my port flushed. I so comfortable with the nurses at the cancer center I decided to go there to have it taken care of. I made a short phone call to tell them I was coming. They said to just come on over, and as soon as someone got a minute, they would flush it and I could be on my way. That is what I did, and it only took a few minutes.

The following week a friend of ours called and invited us to have dinner with them on Friday evening at the Saloon and Grill in WaKeeney. We met them about 6:30 that evening, and it was the first time since my treatment they had seen me. They seemed surprised how good I looked. We ordered a nice meal and had a good visit. When we got up to leave, I grabbed David's arm and told him I felt lightheaded, so he sat me down at an empty chair close to the door. I thought I was feeling a little better, so we got up to leave again. I got as far as the door, and I passed out right in the front door. That is not the worst part. In my passed-out state, I vomited a couple of times in my own lap. My friend Kathy yelled into the restaurant, "Call 911, Anita just passed out."

As I awoke, the ambulance pulled up. There were a couple

of policemen, the EMT, a driver and a couple of other people. I felt so embarrassed, but there was nothing I could do about it. They loaded me into the ambulance and off we went to the hospital ER. Kathy quickly thought of my messy clothing, and not knowing if I was going home or spending the night in the hospital, she made a stop at Dollar General and got me a clean shirt and a pair of capris, which was very thoughtful.

The doctor on call quickly came in to assess my situation and decided to keep me in the hospital to try to get my stomach to calm down and give me fluids. The nurse came in to start an IV and I told him to use my port, he said he would. He went to get the supplies and started to insert the needle and seemed to have some trouble, I asked him if he got draw back, and he said no, but it will be fine. I didn't think it was right, it just didn't feel right to me, after all, it was not the first time someone used my port. Well, he went ahead and started the fluids. They gave me some medicine to calm my stomach and something to help me sleep. The nurse took me to my room and I was getting really sleepy so David, Bob and Kathy left for the night.

I fell asleep shortly thereafter, but I didn't stay asleep very long, as my port area was hurting. Well, the nurse did miss the port. I had a softball size pocket of fluids around my port, not in it. I quickly called for help, and he came in. I said, "I told you it wasn't right." Instead of trying the port again, he just put it in my arm, after he had asked me if I was right or left-handed. I told him I was very right-handed, so what did he do—put the IV in the inside the elbow on my right arm. What an idiot.

The rest of the night passed without another incident, I slept pretty well. The next morning, the PA came in, and she decided to continue what the doctor the night before decided to do until my regular doctor came in on Monday to check things out. I think, her knowing I was a cancer patient kind of scared her.

A new nurse came in and asked why I had the IV in my arm instead of using my port. He said it would be more comfortable. I told him the story, and he assured me he would hit it the first time. I agreed, so he put the IV in my port instead of my arm. He was right, he did hit it the first time, and it was definitely more comfortable, as I knew it would be. My family came to see me, as well as a few of my friends, and everyone had a good laugh when I told them the story of why I was in the hospital. I'm not sure what medicine they gave me for my stomach, but I was not vomiting anymore, it decided to leave by the "back door" and I mean it wanted out in a hurry, so then I had diarrhea.

Monday finally came and so did the doctor. He decided to keep me on the medicine for a couple of weeks and if things cleared up I should be fine. He said I could go home tomorrow if I had a good night. My night was fine, the diarrhea let up some, and after the doctor came in, he allowed me to go home. David came to take me home, it is always good to be at home when you don't feel well.

It was the first day of the Trego County Free Fair, so David would be busy all week barbequing pork burgers for the FFA Alumni pork burger food stand. I had been in charge of this stand for the past seven years, so it was hard for me to turn it over to someone who had no clue what I had been doing. I decided I should not go out to be around people since my immune system was not very strong. That Saturday was supposed to be my forty-fifth-class reunion, but of course I was not able to go because of my depressed immune system. David left each morning about 8:00 a.m., and not be home until about 11:00 p.m., so I spent the entire day at home alone trying to get better. I thought I was having an allergic reaction to the medicine the doctor gave me, but I didn't want David to worry because he is so busy with the fair and all. I would have him take me to the medical clinic on Monday after things slowed down for him.

Monday finally came and we went to the medical clinic. Dr. DeAndrade came in to check me out and he agreed that the symptoms I had were definitely a reaction to the medicine. He decided to let me try to get along without any more medicine since I now had so many allergies. If I didn't seem to get better, he would try something else. As the days went by, I did start to feel better, so I really think it was just a reaction to my last chemo treatment and eating too much of a good thing that night we went out.

Another month went by and it was port flushing time again. I had talked with the girls at Wellness, and they told me there were a few nurses who knew how to access a port without messing it up. So I thought I would give it a try and see if someone could flush it without missing. Linda was my nurse the first time I went into the out-patient clinic to get the port flushed. She was good and knew how to access it. That was good to know so I don't have to make a trip to Hays every time. The next time I had to flush my port would be when I got my CT, so I will go to Hays and have them flush, and then leave the pigtail in for the CT so I don't have to get poked twice.

The month went by really fast, but that was not a bad thing. I was really stressing about the results of my upcoming tests. I so want them to be good with no more active cancer cells. If there was just scar tissue that would be good, but I still had trouble catching my breath. I knew that worrying about what would come wasn't good, but I just couldn't stop my thoughts. When I went to bed and tried to fall asleep, I could not stop my mind from wondering and doing the "what ifs."

I was starting to get my appetite back, sometimes I just wanted to eat and eat, but of course eating has always been a comfort for me, so when I worry I eat, which is not always a good thing. It had almost been three months since my last treatment and my hair was coming back, it was a little darker than before, but the back was coming back really curly. My hair felt so funny. I have always had very straight hair and now it was kinky curly. I wondered as it grew, would it continue to be curly or would it grow out to be straight again.

The CT was tomorrow and I was really worried about the outcome. I sat in my chair and started to say a prayer to ask God to help me get through this. I leaned back and closed my eyes and I felt a really warm and soft loving hug, I could not open my eyes and a voice very calmly said to me that everything would be fine, don't worry I will get you through this. A few seconds later I could open my eyes, I sat up in my chair and it was then that I knew that Jesus was holding me and telling me that things would be fine. That was the first time I ever had a vision like that, and I immediately had no more fear about the tests I was to have the next day.

Test day came and went. CTs really don't take very long but waiting for the results does take a long time. Since I am not very patient I decided to sign up on the patient portal from Hays Medical Center, that way I could see my test results and prepare myself for my doctor's visit when I officially found out the results. Well I did get on the portal and find my results, but I really did not understand for sure how to read it. I will ask a lot of questions so next time I will understand what they are saying.

Three days later I sat in the doctor's office waiting for Dr. Rodriguez. He came in with a smile, and I just knew it was good news. He always remembered something special about me and made mention of it each time. His thing to always remember was my nails and how pretty they looked and made mention of them. He visited a little bit and finally gave me the report I was waiting for. Things looked really good, the tumor seems to be a mass of scar tissue, and everything seems to be normal. He decided that next month I would have a PET Scan done to make sure there were no little green critters running around, which meant no active cancer cells. He would report at our next meeting. He said to continue flushing the port just in case we needed the port at a later date. That is not what I wanted to hear. I thought I would get it taken out, but I understood why we needed to leave it active, just in case.

Next month same procedure, go in for a flush, but the PET Scan guy didn't want to use the port, he liked to put the radioactive stuff in my vein. So after the flush we went to have the scan. It still freaks be out to think that there is radioactive stuff running around inside my body. I just needed to remember to drink a lot of water to flush it out as soon as possible. Just a couple of days later I went to see the doctor to find out what the scan showed. When Dr. Rodriguez came in with that big grin on his face, I knew that as of that point I was cancer free!!! The plan now was to have a CT every three months and follow up with a doctor's appointment, and of course flush my port every four weeks. The Lyrica really wasn't working for my neuropathy, so he prescribed another medicine that I took three times a day instead of once. I gave it a try.

Christmas would soon be here again and it would be so good to see all the kids and grandkids. I hoped to have enough energy to pull it all together, but I knew with the kids help I could manage it all. Clayton was getting to be such a nice-looking man, well-mannered and such a good hugger, and Dustin was following not far behind. All the kids and grands are very affectionate, and that made me feel so good to get those hugs. We had a good meal and gathered around the Christmas tree to open presents. Allison was helping Delaney with her new things and danced around the living room as girls do. It was so wonderful to have them all home for Christmas and hard to see them leave again to live their normal lives.

Chapter Six

TESTING EVERY THREE MONTHS

Accept changes in life gracefully.

January 2016. I can't believe it has been a year since the whole cancer thing has started. Hard to believe I have lived through this whole thing. I had just found out the doctors didn't think I would live through the first round of chemo and radiation. They had said that it was going to be a rough ride, and they were not kidding. I guess I am just a tough old bird and they just didn't know how tough I really was. I try not to think about dying and not ever seeing my family again or being there for all the special times in their lives, but I am too busy concentrating on living to dwell on dying.

I asked Dr. Rodriguez if I would be able to have my eye surgery now that I was not in treatment, and he said it would be fine. I decided to give Dr. Varenhorst, the retinal specialist, a call to set up an appointment. I called and they set up an appointment for the following week on Wednesday at 10:00 a.m. I sure didn't want to start on the next week stuff again, I hoped he could do it right away without waiting until the next week.

The next Wednesday came, and we had to get up and leave early to make the 10:00 appointment. The trip alone was three and a half hours to Wichita and then another half hour through traffic to make it to the office on time. We made it with time to spare, and of course we had to wait about forty-five minutes for my call back to see the doctor. Dr. Varenhorst said that he could remove the part of the retina that had flagged up into my line of sight, and I would be able to see. The only problem he saw was the retina itself had wrinkled and due to the length of time since it happened, he didn't know if it would straighten out on its own and he could not fix the wrinkle. I asked him how soon he could do the procedure, and he said he usually does surgeries on Thursdays, so he could set it up for the following Thursday. I asked if he could do it tomorrow, it was Thursday. He alluded to the fact that I would have to stay over and asked if I was really prepared to stay. I told him if he could do it, I would stay and have it done. He said to let him look to see what he could do. He came back and asked if I could be there by 7:00 a.m. I told him if you can do it, I will be there.

As soon as I left the doctor's office, I called my cousin Toni and asked if I could spend the night so I could have my eye surgery in the morning. She quickly responded with, "How soon will you be here?" We arrived at Toni's house in about fifteen minutes and told her what was going on. David decided he needed to go home and come back the next morning, so he could do the chores and get a change of clothes, since we would have to stay the next night as well, and go back for a checkup the next morning. I decided to run to Wal-Mart and get a change of clothes for the next day, and David could bring me some for the following.

After David left, Toni and I had a good visit, but I had to get to bed so I could be ready for my surgery the next day. The morning came quickly, and we went to the hospital. I checked in and got ready for the procedure which I hoped would allow me to see again out of my right eye. Toni volunteers at that hospital. Everyone knew her and said she was one of the good ones, but I already knew that, it was nice to hear it anyway.

The doctor can in and said he was ready to do the procedure. He asked if I had any questions. No questions, just ready to get it over with. The nurse got me ready and took me back. The doctor came in and told me I would be awake for the whole procedure, he was just going to sedate my right eye and cover the left one. I was able hear everything that was said, but I could not feel a thing or see what they were doing. He made three tiny incisions and removed the part of the retina that had torn away. Then he put a patch on my eye, and it was over. It did not take very long at all, and I was ready to go. David arrived before I was back in the recovery room with Toni. We left and went back to Toni's. We spent the night there again so I could go to my post procedure appointment the next day.

My appointment was at 10:00 the next morning, and it was a positive appointment. The doctor said that everything went fine, and when they removed the patch I could see out of my right eye. Man what a relief. The only thing he could not say was whether the waviness of the retina would smooth out, only time would tell. A cataract would probably develop in a short time, as soon as six months. There was really nothing he could do about either one of those conditions, but at least I could see. If I kept both eyes open I saw fine, if I closed my left eye, I saw everything with a waving motion, kind of weird, but I could live with that, I just kept both eyes open.

Now that my eye was fixed, I needed to go to the dentist to see if the chemo has messed with my teeth. Chemo changed my life in so many ways, my hair fell out, and I'm surprised my teeth didn't. I was a little scared to go and have things checked out, but I felt that I needed to. I didn't think there was any problem, but one never knows for sure. I did get an appointment quickly, it would be next week. Next week came quite quickly and things checked out. Luckily I had no problems with my teeth, and that was a good thing.

Time seemed to be flying by, I kept busy now that I didn't have to go to treatments every day. I really felt pretty good, so I started back to work at Gibson's a couple days a week or whenever they called me. I went to Wellness on Tuesday and

Thursday mornings, the exercise and camaraderie were both good for me, and of course I had to have my port flushed every four weeks.

The more I got out the better I felt, I think it was because I could keep my mind busy and not dwell on my illness. Most of the time people saw me they did ask how I was doing, and they all said I looked good. My hair started growing back, it was still very short, but it covered the baldness. There were always questions about how the cancer made me feel. I told them that the cancer itself never made me feel bad, or sick, the only way I knew something was wrong was the cough I had, but my treatment made me sick.

The editor of our local newspaper called me one day to ask if we had finished my studio and were ready for her to do a story on me and my handcrafted jewelry. I told her the studio was finished and it would be wonderful to have her do an interview and give me some publicity for my craft.

WESTERN KANSAS WORLD

MARCH 17, 2016
Nita's Nest is Open

Everyone in the WaKeeney area knows Anita Schneider. Her involvement in the FFA Alumni has spanned over a decade and included not only the local and stare, but also the national level. She and her husband, Dave, have played their guitars and provided music at many events. They have been involved in many things throughout the community.

In recent years, beautiful jewelry made of natural stones has appeared in stores and on Facebook, as well as being worn by many individuals. Each piece is unique and one-of-a-kind and yes they are "Nita's Notions."

Anita can tell you what each stone is and share with you its properties and qualities. Each piece is wire wrapped to set off the stone to its highest advantage.

The stones are found in a variety of places. Some are found locally, some are ordered or gathered up at markets. Anita studies the stones to decide how they should be used and then Dave takes the larger stones and cuts them how and where they are needed.

Anita said she started her "hobby gone wild" at one of her sister-get-togethers. She and her three sisters always brought projects to do at these sister fests. Sister Irene was the instigator of the wire-wrapping with all of the girls eventually getting involved. Anita said she wasn't initially sold of the subject because she was always trying to make the pieces perfect.

But once Anita discovered that it was the imperfections and irregularities that made them spectacular, she was off and running. At first she gave her jewelry as gifts, but requests kept coming in for her pieces, and sales began.

In January of 2015, the jewelry creations were put on hold, when Anita was diagnosed with Adenocarcinoma, an abnormal lung cancer, and in April she began treatments in Hays. After several months of treatments, scans showed clear in both August and November. It was with great joy that the doctors finally delivered the news they believed they had it all.

Anita's face appeared again at Gibson's Health Mart where she is employed part-time. New jewelry pieces started popping up, too.

In January, a pre-fab structure appeared on the Schneider's farm, the inside was completed, and set up as a workshop for Anita to make and display her creations and just recently "Nita's Nest" opened to the public.

The Nest is big enough for Anita to hold small classes where small groups can come in and learn how to make their own pieces. She already has Scouts lined up for a class and she is open for making reservations for other groups. Just call 785-769-4452.

Recently Anita has been called in for more tests to determine the cause of a coupled of new spots. She has just returned from KU, but will not hear results until later in March. Prayers are appreciated for positive results from these tests and ever increasing good health for Anita. We are wanting Anita to have many more hours of pleasure in creating her pieces from her Nest.

Sidebar: The name "Nita's Nest" comes from David raising chickens on his farm which they sometimes lovingly call the chicken farm.

Cathy Millard

March arrived and it was CT time. It had only been three months and I was really nervous about what they might find. I would have my CT on Wednesday and wouldn't see the Oncologist until the next Wednesday, but I would look on the website to see what they found. Sometimes I could make out the reports but it would only be confirmed when I saw the doctor. The week before the test I always thought about what they may find, the nights were always the hardest, just can't stop the thoughts and the "what ifs." Then the week between test and appointment was another hard time for me. That was when the prayers really seem to come. The CT appointment went off without a hitch, then just the wait for the reports.

When Dr. Rodrigues comes in he is always so pleasant, but this time I was not able to read his expressions. I just had to wait for him to tell me what the reports confirm. My blood work all looked good, lungs sounded strong, and as he took a look at the report I took a deep breath. "Well, things don't look perfect. There is a small growth on your left adrenal gland, and I'm not sure what to think. I think we will just watch it for the next three months and do another CT to see if it grows in size." As soon as he said there was a small growth, my eyes started to tear up., He told me there was nothing to worry about, yet. Another deep breath and still the tears ran down my face. He looked at me and said, "Don't worry. I will let you know when you need to worry, and I don't want you to be upset." He asked if I need something for depression.

I said, "No, I just need to come to grips what you just told me, then I will be fine. It will take me a minute to adjust, then I will be okay.

"If you change your mind, I am here for you and can get you something."

David and I walked out of the office hand in hand and he said to me "Don't worry, you'll be alright." I was quiet the rest of the way home, not knowing for sure what was to come. Now I had a new thing to worry about for the next three months. If it was for sure a new tumor, then I go directly to stage four, which means that it was metastatic and would be on treatment forever. I guess I needed to pray a little harder for God to protect me, and help me through this.

The next three months were about the same as the last three; work a bit at Gibson's, Wellness twice a week, port flush every four weeks, and the weather was nice, so I started golfing again. The ladies golf was on Tuesdays. So right after Wellness I went golfing, and that was such fun, and I loved to visit with the ladies. June would be here before I knew it and I prayed to God that the growth has not changed.

I got my CT and doctor appointments in the mail, and that was when the worrying kicked in again. *When you wait, every time you get an ache or pain, your thoughts always seem to go to what if it is another tumor, or has my cancer started to grow again?* It really didn't matter what kind of feeling out of the ordinary I had, it immediately went to negative thoughts of cancer. I didn't do the *why me?*, because cancer can hit anyone. A friend of mine thought that he had cancer, but it turned out to be a rare disease. He was convinced God gave him that trial as a punishment for the kind of life he had been living. But I know deep in my heart that God is not a punishing or vengeful God, he is a forgiving and a loving God. He was there to help me get through this trial, not to punish me. He was there to make me stronger in my faith, maybe to help someone else to get through a trial. I just don't know for sure, but I am here because he was helping me to live through this and grow closer to Him.

CT scan day came and I hoped and prayed the reports would be good and I would know in just a few days. David took me to the cancer center to get my port flushed and they left a pigtail in to get the contrast injected. We only had to wait a few minutes for the port to be accessed and then we took the long walk through the tunnels of the hospital to get to the radiology department. Usually the same person took me in for the test, and we had a nice visit on our walk reminding me of the process for the test and had a laugh or two. We stopped and had a bite to eat after the test because I was not supposed to eat before. I got to choose, and IHOP was always a good place to eat.

Doctor appointment was on Wednesday and we drove to the cancer center in Hays for my reports. Weight, blood pressure, temperature check, and a few questions and then we waited for Dr. Rodriguez, which was only a few minutes but seemed longer, because of my anticipation for my reports. He came in and checked my nails, but his expression was hard to read that time so that made me anxious. He did the heart check and said the blood work looked good--then the CT report. "Well, it is not as good as I wish it was, the small growth on the adrenal gland has grown, not a lot, but it has grown. So I want to have it biopsied and see what we are looking at, if it is a cancer tumor or a benign growth. We will set that up next week and I will see you back here, the following week." My eyes welled up again and Doc said, "Don't worry. I will get you through this, we just have to find out what we are dealing with."

The day for the biopsy came quickly. My appointment was at 9:00, at the Hays Hospital. No eating or drinking after midnight, so I was glad it was early. I went to the radiology department and into the CT room. The Radiologist told me to lie on my stomach. They gave me a little pain medicine and he put me in the scanner to actually see where the tumor was. Then insert a biopsy needle into the growth and extract some tissue. I lay there and the doctor told me to take a breath, blow it out and hold, don't breathe. He began inserting the needle and the pain was unreal, he tried to continue and the pain was excruciating, so that I couldn't even begin to take a breath. He tried again and oh my, the pain was unbearable. The doctor said, "I give up, I can't do this."

So I got dressed and headed out to the waiting room to tell David what happened. When I got to the waiting room David knew that something went wrong because of the tears rolling down my face. That appointment was a big waste of time and money, I bet they charged me for the radiologist's unsuccessful attempt. David couldn't believe what had just happened, and how weird the radiologist was about throwing up his hands in failure.

At my appointment with Dr. Rodriguez the following week and he could not believe the story of the futile attempt either. He told me that he would never put me through anything like that again, from now on he would have me go to KU Medical Center in Kansas City for biopsies. He had a classmate that he knew would be gentler, more thorough and get a sample for testing. Well you guessed it—my appointment was next week at KU Med for my biopsy, and had an appointment with Dr. Rodriguez the next week.

I called Joshua on our way home and asked if he would be home next weekend and able to take me to KU for my tests on Monday morning at 10:00. He said he would do both and couldn't wait to see us. He was more than happy to take me to my appointment. We decided to go to Kansas City on Friday, so we could spend a couple days with the kids. The six-hour trip seemed to go by quickly and it was so good to see the kids. Delaney is such a sweet little girl, she was getting so that she ran to us and those hugs felt so good. We had such a good time playing some of the little "girl" things that Delaney liked to play, like store, mom and baby, kitchen and fun--things like that, she was a hoot.

Monday came way too soon. I was so glad Joshua could take us to KU since I had no clue where it was. He definitely knows his way around Kansas City, as well as the hospital, since he works at one. He worked at KU during his college years when he was doing his practical in radiology. I checked in and it was only a short time until they came to get me ready for the biopsy. Joshua went back with me for my prep to make sure I got a staff doctor, not a resident. Since this was a teaching hospital, if you don't specifically say you want staff, you can get a resident, and he did not want that. They took me back to the CT scanner, gave me a shot and the next thing I knew, I was waking up in my room. Wow, was that different than the guy at Hays, I didn't feel a thing and he did get tissues to test.

It was hard to leave the kids the next day, but Joshua had to go to work, and David needed to get home too. I was great to see the kids and play with Delaney, we don't get to see them all that often and I missed that. Even though I was a little down about why I went to KC, I had to make the best of it and tried not to think about me and my problems. The trip home went by fast for me—I slept most of the way, so David just kept driving and did not stop until we got home.

Now I had to wait another week for my next appointment to find out the result. Where would we go from here—*cancer again, treatment, metastatic, finally getting my hair back and will I lose it again, feeling bad, surgery, new doctor?* Not knowing was so hard, if you knew, you could deal with it. Random thoughts as usual when things are unknown.

Chapter Seven

METASTATIC

Remember that today is the first day of the rest of your life.

My grandson, Dustin asked me to go to Europe with him and the Ambassadors of Music, as he had been selected by his vocal instructor to be a part of this group and share his talent. I so wanted to go, but I told him I really didn't think I could go because I didn't know what I would have to have done with the new tumor that had been diagnosed. He couldn't wait any longer because he had to have the paperwork in by the fifteenth of June. He was disappointed but understood. I was very disappointed; it was a real honor just to have him ask me to share this experience with him.

The day finally came, and I really needed David to come with me. I was afraid of what the results would tell. I was right, the test did find this growth was indeed a tumor, it was cancerous and we would need to do something. Dr. Rodriguez sent me to a Urologist, Dr. Lopez, who would do the removal procedure. We had a preliminary visit to check things out and together we decided when it could be done. A couple days later the Urology clinic called and my appointment was set up for next week.

Off to Hays again, this time to see a new doctor, Dr. Lopez the Urologist. I had never been to a Urologist before so I really didn't know what to expect. The nurse called me back, handed me a urine cup, and told me to go into a rest room and give her a sample. That was the first time I ever had that happen, but I gave her what she had asked for and proceeded to follow her into the exam room. Temperature and blood pressure I expected, but not a sonogram, which was the order of things. After the sonogram she told me my bladder was not quite empty. I'm thought to myself, *This is a little weird, but I guess that is the way things are done here.*

Dr. Lopez came in and introduced himself and shook our hands. He was so young, but when you get as old as I am everybody now days in the medical profession is young. He was very nice. He took another look at my reports and said what he wanted to do. The tumor seemed to be totally encased in the adrenal gland so, he would remove the entire gland by using the laparoscopic method. Four small incisions would be made through my abdomen and he would remove the affected adrenal gland from the front. It was a lot less aggressive than traditional surgery, and healing time was minimal. That sounded good to me, I just had to remember that the healing was on the inside, so I would need to be careful not to overexert. I was to stop upfront and have the gal set up the time for the procedure, which would be next Wednesday. They would call me on Tuesday about the time.

I had been dealing with cancer for almost two years and never felt bad except for when I was in chemotherapy treatment. I did not had any pain, symptoms, or a warning of any kind that I had cancer. The cancer became metastatic and I was going to have a surgical procedure to remove another tumor. Still no warning, this is why so many people are diagnosed with cancer when it is too late and not treatable. I am so glad that I had that nagging cough and got it checked out before it was too late., Because even though I had to go through all this stuff, it was still better than finding it when it was so far advanced and nothing could be done.

The call on Tuesday informed us to be there by 7:00 in the morning for the procedure. I am not sure, but I was not very nervous about the procedure, maybe it was because I had been through so much already that I just thought it couldn't be any worse. I usually took sedation quite well, with very minimal side effects, and this time wasn't any different, went to sleep, procedure was done, and woke up without any complications.

I had only four small band aids and no pain at all, just a little excess air in my abdominal cavity. Dr. Lopez came in to be sure things were okay and see if I had any questions. He said that he was very sure that he got it all, but we would have to wait until the tests results come back to be sure he got all the margins. My follow up appointment with him was next week Wednesday. He told me to take it easy for this week and not lift, no quick movements, and don't drive until I see him, and at that time he will have my appointment set with Dr. Rodriguez who will tell me the results and recommendations on how to proceed.

My follow up appointment was quite uneventful, everything seemed to be healing nicely and I could resume normal activities. The next appointment with my Oncologist was the one I worried about. I really didn't want to have another round of chemo, but if he recommended that I have chemo, I guessed that was what I would do. I came this far trusting him, guess I would continue to trust. I had another thought. *I don't have chemo would they be able to remove my port? That would be a positive thing, it would mean that they do not think I would need it again.* Unanswered questions, unknown things again were the thoughts my mind seemed to wonder into, you know the "what ifs" game. Most people, when you talk about cancer think about the physical side of the disease, but for me the mental side was hard, you can treat the cancer tumors, but you can't stop your thoughts.

The appointment with my Oncologist came to find out the test results and how we would proceed. I was so anxious to find out the results, and quite nervous at the same time, I wanted to know and I didn't want to know, fear was not my friend. I know my blood pressure was rising as I waited for the doctor to come in. There was a tap on the door, Dr. Rodriguez came in, but I not could read his expression, so I took a deep breath and waited.

He went through his regular routine, asking me some questions about how I was feeling, listened to my heart and lungs, and then sat down with the reports in his hands. I took another deep breath and asked him if the reports were good or bad. He looked at me and said, "The tumor was cancerous, but it was entirely encased in the adrenal gland and they got all the margins when it was removed." He then told me that we will not have to do any chemo or any other treatment. We would continue to do CTs every three months to be sure nothing else showed, and we would also continue to flush the port, so that if we ever needed it, we kept it in good working order. He set up a follow up appointment just after the CT was completed, Trudy would send me the information after she set up the times.

Oh what a relief, no chemo, just CTs to watch for any new developments. Since it was metastatic, there was a good chance the cancer would show its ugly head again. We would just have to hope and pray that it doesn't show up again.

Three months until I had to do anything but a flush every month, so I was going to try not to think about what could happen. I was going to live life to the fullest and take one day at a time. Thanksgiving and Christmas were coming, so no time for worry. Holidays are always good for us, family always seems to enjoy each other, and if I do say so myself, the food seems to be a hit each year. For some reason the kids always want to come home for the holidays, they say it just isn't a holiday if they don't come home. I'm fine with that, I enjoy it when they come and that year was special because of the tough last two years I had, and for now I am cancer free.

It was sometime after lunch, after we unwrapped presents and were just hanging out and visiting, when Dustin pulled me aside and said he had something to ask me. That seemed really serious for him to do this. He asked me if I was well enough to go to Europe with him and the group. I told him that if he could still get me in, I would love to go with him. I thought to myself, There is no way, our reservations were to be in the last of June, and here it is the last of December, but if he can get me in I'll do it.

Chapter Eight

KEEP THE FAITH

Keep hope alive within your heart.
Seeking refuge each day, from a higher power above,
knowing His love is the way.

It was January 2017, and I was feeling good and optimistic for the future. I had come so far. No matter what I was not going to give up, I was going to stay positive and take one day at a time. The last three months went by so fast and it was time for a CT and an appointment with my Oncologist. I went for my CT on Wednesday and to my surprise I had a reaction to the contrast dye that they injected in my blood stream to enable for them to see what is going on. I stopped by the drug store on my way home from Hays, and Bernita said I had a weird red spot on my left cheek. She said to watch it to be sure that wasn't the start of a reaction. I watched it off and on for the next few hours and it continued to get larger. My entire face got red and very hot. That seemed so strange, I put ice packs on my face for the next couple of days, and it got very uncomfortable. My uvula got quite inflamed and swollen, so I knew that it was a reaction and I needed to talk to Dr. Rodriguez about it when I saw him, next week. I talked to Bernita about it and she said that if I continued to have the dye it would get worse each time I was given it. That seemed quite scary to me and hoped there was something that could be done.

The following Wednesday was my appointment with Dr. Rodriguez, and he said that he had good news for me, there was no new tumors showing on the test. I told him about my reaction and he was surprised that it took so long to show up, usually within a couple minutes it begins to show. I guess I really do not follow the rules, I am a unique person and do my own thing. He said that he would prescribe a pretreatment regiment to be taken prior to my next CT scan. I talked to him about going to Europe with my grandson and he thought that it was a great idea if we could work it out. If something showed up beforehand, we would just wait until I got back and deal with it then. That sounded good to me, just so Dustin could work it out.

Dustin called me a few days later and said that he explained the situation to them, and they said that they would work it out so I could go. I was so excited to go, when they sent me the paperwork I returned it with my fee immediately. He is quite a kid, to want Grandma to go with him on a twenty-day trip to Europe, I could hardly wait until June and we get to go. In April we attended an informational meeting and ordered jackets and the choir shirts. The choir started their practice. These kids were awesome, cream of the crop and so talented. They also set up another practice in a month. It would be all practice time, Friday, Saturday from eight until six each day, and a shorter day on Sunday. There would be a concert Sunday evening for anyone who wanted to come, kind of a dress rehearsal.

The next time we went was just a few days prior to our trip to Europe, and Dustin caught the conductor one morning prior to rehearsal and told her that his grandma could sing. She then asked me if I would be willing to sing with the kids. I told her that I didn't order a shirt and I didn't pack any black dress pants or shoes. She told me I could purchase one of her shirts because it was too small for her, and if I wanted, I could purchase shoes and slacks to wear prior to us leaving. I was so excited to be able to sing in seven different countries in Europe that I had to say yes and go shopping for slacks and shoes. I'm a fast shopper, and I only missed part of the first rehearsal. Then I was ready to participate, thanks to Dustin.

That night when I went to spend the night with Toni, I told her what he had done, and she was about as excited as I was. Toni, David, Jason, Chris and Clayton came to the concert and brought the rest of our clothes and said good-bye. David drove us to Kansas City to meet the plane the next day. We spent the night with Joshua, Kay and Delaney, so we could also tell them good-bye., David took us to the airport and then headed for home.

With everything that had gone on in my life in the last couple of years, I couldn't believe I was on my way to Europe. But I just I decided I did not know how long I would be able to do something like that and having the opportunity to spend time with my grandson was priceless. I may never have another chance come along. The people on this trip were wonderful, the adults were firm but fair, and the kids included me in with them. Dustin was great keeping an eye on Grandma and being sure that I was never left alone or needed anything. We did a lot of walking and my neuropathy could be quite painful, but I just wore my supportive shoes and did my best to keep up.

We visited England, France, Switzerland, Liechtenstein, Austria, Italy and Germany. The group toured many known places and interesting sites, castles, cathedrals, Notre Dame, Matterhorn, and Eiffel tower. We stayed in hotels and hostels, and we saw the changing of the guard and enjoyed much local cuisine. We performed in some advertised sites and cathedrals that had awesome acoustics. Our conductor would just tell us to gather, and we would sing. We didn't carry music as it was all memorized.

It was a trip I will never forget, and the time I spent with Dustin and all the wonderful people was priceless. Wherever we went, the people were so kind and welcoming. This program had groups from all over the United States tour at different times. There was a group from Texas that arrived as we were leaving.

The upcoming time change made the jet lag a little easier to get used to, we went back in time and relived about eight hours. I was sure I would need those hours for sleep. I would be so excited to tell all about our trip that it would be hard to get some needed rest, but the trip was so worth every minute. I purchased a special bottle of a butterscotch liquor for Clayton, and he thought that was great. He drank the drink and saved the bottle. I took so many pictures and even some video of the choir singing that will be fun to share.

With only a couple days after getting back from Europe to get ready for my upcoming CT, I had to jump back into reality quickly. I needed to take the first dose of medicine the morning prior to the appointment, second dose evening before, and then last dose the morning of the CT. One hour before my appointment I also needed to drink the Breeza which was also a contrasting agent, then head off to Hays.

The CT itself went off without a hitch but the next few hours was a totally different story. It was about four hours when I began to show signs of an allergic reaction. There was a spot on my left cheek just below my eye, a red spot appeared and the redness continued until my entire face was bright red and really hot to the touch. My face was uncomfortably hot to the touch as well a very hot feeling on the inside. It felt like a very bad sunburn. I was so glad that the last time I had a reaction I had ordered an ice face mask. The ice pack on my face did feel more comfortable, but the ice didn't last very long. My face was so hot that it only took about fifteen minutes until the ice melted and had to be put back into the freezer. I let it freeze for two hours then placed it back on my face. I continue to do this through the entire day, and one time before going to bed.

I awoke the next morning with difficulty breathing, so

I hurried to get ready to head to the emergency room. My breathing was labored, and I felt my throat was closing up. Sure enough I was in antihelixes, the ER doc gave me a shot of epinephrine to reduce the swelling and help me breathe more comfortably. Man, what a feeling that shot gave me, my heart was pounding so hard and I was jittery. It was the weirdest thing I had ever experienced. The good thing was it worked. It didn't take too long before I could breathe normally and was able to go home in just a couple hours. The doctor told me that I should not use the injectable dye again, each time the symptoms would get worse. I was certain that Dr. Rodriguez was not going to want to hear news that the pretreatment did not work.

My appointment was with him next week and I was not sure what he would decide to do. Joshua works in radiology and deals with this kind of things also, so I thought I would give him a call to see what he would do in a case like this. He sees many more patients than they do in Hays. I called him and he said to try doubling the pretreatment dose and see if that helped. I suggested that to the doctor to see what he thought, it wasn't going to hurt anything I thought.

The day to see if there was anything new in my scan came, and I was afraid of what they found. I don't know why, I just had a feeling that it wasn't going to be good. It seemed that something new always showed up about every three months and three months have passed. I got to the cancer center and had all the preliminary work up, and I wait to see the doctor. Of course, I was nervous to find out. Well my suspicions were right. There were a couple of lymph nodes in the abdominal anterior that have grown. The doctor was not certain they grew enough to be concerned, so he decided, if it was okay with me, to watch them and check again in three months to see if they continued to grow. They were very small but have grown a small amount, and worth a watch. He knew best so we would just watch them at this time.

The next few months I spent a lot of time making new pieces of jewelry so that I would have a good amount to show at my crafts fairs in the fall. The weather was nice so it is a good time to spend time in my studio constructing some new creations.

Chapter Nine

ANOTHER STORM

The days will pass bringing relief,
and don't forget to praise, the blessings bestowed
upon you, a joyful song they raise.

The next few months seemed to fly by, getting ready for the holidays, craft fairs, and of course worrying about the results of my next tests always was in the back of my mind. The first craft fair was the first Saturday in November and I was excited to see how this year went. Last year was stressful with all that was going on in my life at that time. This show was in Hays for "Your Voice through Cancer," and it always seemed to be quite good. I was always happy to see so many of my friends who were also conflicted with this nasty disease known as cancer. The group asked for door prizes to encourage people in, and the more people we had the better our sales should be. I always donated a necklace and earring set--after all the proceeds went to a good cause to help cancer patients with their trials. The day did go quite well, I sold some pieces and got some special orders, and I was more comfortable with my appearance since I have real hair again.

My next fair was in Dodge City, for the Knights of Columbus, it was a two-day fair, Friday afternoon, evening and all-day

Saturday. David, Mari and I drove down and set up on Friday to get things ready. Before we even had things all set up, we had shoppers and that was a good thing. It was our second year there so hopefully people who purchased last year would tell their friends and we would have a good crowd and make a lot of sales. David came with us in case we had vehicle trouble and he is a good salesman. We appreciate his help setting up and tearing down. Saturday night came quickly and the sales went quite well. We tore the display down and were about ready to head home, but first we had to stop and get a bite to eat. I got out of the pick-up and started to walk to McDonald's, and I miss stepped and fell right there in the parking lot. There was a small depression in the asphalt, and I didn't see it and down I went. I hurt my knee, and thought I stretched the muscles in my back, it really started to hurt.

The next few days the pain in my back continued to hurt more and more each day. I decided to go to a chiropractor and see if my back was out of place. The chiropractor got me in the next day. He checked things out and did some adjustments to see if that would help, and he wanted me to come back in a couple of days. I kept the next appointment even though the pain did not get any less. He did some more adjustments and wanted me to go to my regular doctor to see if they would do an x-ray to make sure nothing was cracked or broken. I went to the walk-in clinic to see if they had any ideas on what was going on with my back. I saw one our PAs and she ordered an x-ray and gave me a prescription for some pain killers.

The clinic called me the next day and said that the x-ray did not show anything cracked or broken, so they were not sure why it was so painful and getting worse every day. I kept taking the pain meds with no relief, the pain got so bad I could not sit, lay, or walk and sleep did not happen. I went to the clinic again to see if they had any other ideas on how to find out what was going on with my back. She ordered a CT to see if that would show anything. After waiting a couple days for the results, I was more discouraged all the time, because the CT showed nothing. The doctor decided physical therapy might help me get some relief, so I went three times a week.

The physical therapist tried so hard to get to the root of the problem, but no matter how hard she tried, I just could not get any relief. The pain kept getting worse and nothing they tried seemed to help. The doctor ordered an MRI to see if that would give us any indication as to what was happening. In the meantime, she gave me a different kind of pain medicine, a patch that I wore on my upper back. Opioids are terrible drugs and some of the side effects were almost as bad as the reason for taking them. They caused terrible constipation, so every day I took a stool softener to give me some help with the constipation. Wouldn't you know the MRI did not show anything wrong either.

I knew all the pain I had was not in my head, I was not imagining I was in so much pain. At that point about all I could do was try to walk, sit, and do anything to help with the pain. I cried almost all the time, but of course that didn't help with the pain, but I could not help it. I was just in so much pain, and at that point I wasn't sure I even wanted to live, if I had to live like that.

The doctor decided to get me an appointment with a pain specialist and possibly get an injection to see if that would help the pain. I went to see him and he did give me an injection in my lower back to see if that would help. I kept waiting for the injection to take affect and get some relief, but no matter how long I waited, the relief did not come. At that point I was really discouraged, and absolutely did not know what to do next or where to go to try to get help. Mari had such good luck with a doctor in Denver with her back that I decided to give him a try and see what he had to say. My regular doctor was more than happy to set up an appointment with him because nothing he tried seemed to help and we were at our wits end.

By that time I was using pain patches, as well as oral medication to try to get some relief. The Denver doctor comes to a town about two hours closer, and he agreed to see me in just a week, which worked out well. During all this pain, I still had cancer appointments as well. My most recent CT showed that the small lymph nodes had grown from the last CT and Dr. Rodriguez wanted me to go to KU Medical Center and have them preform a biopsy to see if they were indeed cancerous. My appointments were on opposite ends of the state just a couple days apart, but I made it to both of them to get things checked out.

The Denver doctor's appointment came first. David and I drove to Goodland to see him. He looked at all my tests and checked me over. He thought my issues were coming from the vertebrae located on my waist line, and he wanted me to see a colleague of his in Denver for some pain control shots. I agreed I would give it a try and had him set up the appointment. I had to do something. The pain was so bad I could hardly stand it; all I could do was pray and cry. The following day David and I headed to the eastern side of Kansas for my biopsy.

I was not looking forward to the tests, but I was excited to see my little granddaughter Delaney. The two trips back to back really did a number on my back, the pain was almost unbearable. That time my tests were to be done at a new facility just about five minutes from where Joshua and his family live. The facility just performs special tests so waiting time was very minimal, and everyone was nice and accommodating. We spent a couple days with the kids and had a nice time. I tried so hard not to show how much pain I was in, but Joshua saw right through me. He felt so bad for me, as he could tell how much pain I was in, as well as the worry I had about the new tumors and what was going on with them.

The following week we headed to Denver to see the specialist pain doctor. She had me stop taking all my pain medication so she could get a true reading on my pain level. Going off opioids was a real treat, more pain and withdrawal symptoms, and then riding in a car for five hours. We went to my sister's the day before my appointment so I could get some rest. She would drive me there because she knows her way around much better than I do.

By the time for my appointment, I was in so much pain that I could hardly stand it, couldn't sit, walk, or lay except in the fetal position, I even laid that way on a couple of chairs in the waiting room. The doctor did all her checking and viewed my previous tests, and she decided the pain came from misplacement of the sacroiliac. She gave me a pain shot to see if that would help give me relief. We headed home right after the doctor visit hoping the pain shot would make me comfortable enough to make the trip. Well, that pain shot did not work either, and the doctor told me to go back on the pain medicine. But I had already gone through withdrawal and I was not getting relief from the patch, so I decided to not go back on it.

The holidays just weren't going to be the same, even though the boys and their families will all be home for Christmas. That will be nice. I really didn't know just how I would get through the holidays with all the pain I had-- the preparations, shopping, cleaning, cooking and all the things that go along with having guests. I knew they were all family, but still they are so used to me doing most of the work, and I just didn't know how I could do it all. I might have to ask for help, and that was hard for me. I was sure it would all get done, the boys are always willing to help, and that made me feel that I have raised them right. The daughters-in-law were always willing to help too.

The holidays did come and go without too much trouble, I just had to rest and keep taking my medicines to help control the pain. I just wished it would have given me more relief, and I prayed the doctors would find the cause of the pain and fix it. I had been living with awful pain since November and then it was January 2018. As we went into a new year, I wondered what was to come. *Will they find reason for my pain, be able to fix it, what will the results of the biopsy be, will I have chemo again, if I have chemo will I lose my hair, will I get back to some type of normality? What else will I miss because of my health? I have already missed Clayton's high school graduation.*

The day came to go to the Hays cancer center to find out

results. I really think things will be alright. The routine check in was without a hitch, my blood was good, blood pressure was good and no new meds. I was just finding it hard to wait patiently. Doc came in as his usual happy self and pleasant manner, but when he got out the reports, he looked quite serious. He began by telling me the lymph nodes did not check out so good, the cancer spread into them and they were not removable.

Then he tells me that it was always my decision, but there was something he would like to do. There was a new type of cancer treatment, an immune therapy, and he would like for me to try it, if I qualified for it. The Keytruda works with the immune system to destroy the bad cells and also keeps them from reoccurring. Doc had already checked my numbers to see if I qualified for the insurance. There are ten point that tell whether one qualifies for the insurance to pay it, because there is no way one can pay for it on their own, as it is new and very expensive. He said that I met ten out of the ten points, so I was an excellent candidate for the treatment. I told him if that was what he thought we should do, that was what we would do. He gave me some informational materials for me to read about Keytruda and told me he would set up the infusion, it would probably be a week or so before they got it in. So I guess it was decided, new treatment, the not knowing how my body would react, how often would I have to get it, how long would I be on it, and I still have this awful pain in my lower back, what's a girl to do?

A couple of days later I absolutely could not stand the pain, so I had David take me in to the ER. The doctor on call decided to admit me to the hospital and put me on some IV pain medicine to see if that would help. I was glad my room was a private room because I really didn't want anyone to see me in so much pain. It didn't take long before some of my friends heard I was in the hospital, and they started to come to visit. That was fine because I think they understood the condition I was in and how I was suffering.

The doctor tried so hard to get the pain under control but to no avail, the pain continued and seemed to get worse at times. I pretty much just laid on my side in a fetal position and prayed and cried and tried to be strong when people came in. A couple of days went by and the doctor just couldn't understand why there was no relief and decided to do a CT to see if anything showed up that would give him some answers. Just the same as the last time, the CT showed nothing that they could identify as the problem, but the doctor saw the tumors and panicked and decided to send me to Hays to be near my Oncologist. I told him that I knew about the tumors and we were going to start treatment soon, but he still wanted to send me to Hays and see if they could figure anything conclusive to the pain problem. I agreed and off to Hays I went to another set of doctors.

After a couple of days, a person from physical therapy department came in and asked if she could check me, I told her, "Sure give it a try, everyone else has." She did an exam and asked me if I wanted her to fix the problem and I said absolutely, if any way possible. She did some pushing and pulling and I did all I could to resist and counter pulled and pushed as she instructed me to do. Oh my goodness, it worked!! My sacroiliac was about three quarters of an inch out of whack and she put it back in place, and there was instant relief. Praise the Lord!!! I then had some nerve and muscle issues, as they had been out of place for so long that they couldn't find their counterpart, so she set up for me to have physical therapy for about six weeks at the orthopedic center.

I was then dismissed from the hospital and started withdrawal from all the pain medicine that I had been on. I went to water therapy three times a week and really started to feel good. I couldn't believe that after three months, I was pain free. I do not understand how my sacroiliac could be that much out of place and none of the tests done or specialists I saw could find it. I guess that really didn't matter now, I was fixed and I could focus on my new cancer treatment.

Chapter Ten

NEW HOPE

The storms of life will come and go, but do not
be afraid, stay strong and weather out the strife,
the sun will shine again.

I took the break I needed from the cancer treatment to get my back straightened out, and now it was time to focus on getting the cancer under control again. My first treatment of Keytruda was scheduled and after the long infusions that I was used to with chemo, this thirty-minute session was a breeze. Pretreat and the actual chemical infusion only took a little over an hour. I just hoped it worked with minimal side effects, only time would tell. I had the infusion in the morning. David and I went to lunch and did a little shopping and I felt fine; maybe I wouldn't have much of a reaction. Later that day and the next I was a bit tired and that was all. Doc told me that it wasn't anything like the first chemo I was used to, and he was right, but we would only know how it worked after a bit of time and a few treatments were behind us.

The plan for Keytruda was to have treatment every three weeks, see the doctor every other treatment, and have a CT every three months to see how I got along and how it worked. If my reactions were like the first infusion, it won't be so bad if I have to do this forever. If I developed an allergic reaction to the Keytruda, they would have to try a different medicine.

As time has gone on and years have passed, I am still here, I am doing well and the Keytruda is working. I could stretch this out and go treatment to treatment but that would be boring, not going to say it was all a breeze but it has given me a few more years to spend on God's earth.

Keytruda has been good for me, after receiving this treatment my life went back to a type of normality, I went back to working part time, enjoyed playing golf again, giving guitar lessons, singing for the residents at the Long Term Care unit, playing cards, sharing my cancer experience with other newly diagnosed patients, and just enjoying life again. I am not going to say that I didn't have some rough patches. Every time before a CT, my mind continues to wonder if the cancer will become active again.

I have had so many friends diagnosed with cancer in the past few years and not knowing why there are so many in our small community always makes me wonder if there is something in the earth or just what causes it. After Wanda came to me when I was first diagnosed and helped me understand so many things, I decided I would try to help others as she did. I had one person tell me she felt so guilty because she would think about herself during her trials, and I assured her that there was no one more important than she was at that moment in time, she needed to have the want and desire to love and care for herself and be positive about wanting to live. I found out that someone was diagnosed and she didn't want anyone to know so I went to her for a heart to heart. Support is such a positive thing for people to have, knowing that people care about you and pray for you is so important, everyone needs someone. You should never fight alone!

A couple of friends found the reactions to chemotherapy something they just did not want to put themselves through and asked me how I could do it. I assured them that the path they choose whether it be chemo or holistic medicine is their choice, and no one should ever put a negative into their choice, all people need positive support, not tell them that they are making the wrong decision. Just because I chose conventional treatment doesn't mean that their choices are wrong. If it works for them and they feel good about it, support is what they need, not negativity.

A friend was diagnosed with a cancer I really did not know much about. So while we talked, I asked questions and that made her feel I cared, because I did. I could research what I didn't know, so I could understand what she was going through. Even though our cancers were different there were many similarities in the reactions to the treatments. Support and understanding are so very important. She was feeling so bad about her husband feeling so helpless, which is another part of the guilt feeling we can have. The supporting spouse can really struggle with all the things the person they love is going through, and the helplessness they feel is very frustrating for them. What the patient is going through is so real, but so are the feelings the spouse has. The patient needs to assure the supporting spouse that just being there for them is what they need, let the doctors do the treatments.

I have had the supporting person come to me and ask for help on how they can help their loved one. One gentleman was frustrated with his wife's shortness with him and the negativity she portrayed. I told him to be patient with her. Support was what he needed to do to help her be positive and overlook her shortcomings. Just give love and support.

I have had people say to me they would never have chemo and would just let nature take its course. I told them to never say what you would or would not do until they are diagnosed with cancer and are forced to make that decision. Then and only then should they say what they will or will not do. Someone who is not a cancer patient, or even if they are, should never put negativity into a person's decision making as to what they are doing, or where they are going for help. People need support not negative suggestions, or to hear they are wrong on the path they have decided to take in their cancer journey.

One of the hardest things I had to do during my battle was sing at couple of cancer patients' funerals. And what made it really hard was the funerals were almost back to back, they were only two weeks apart. When the surviving family thinks enough of you, to do something like that, there is no way I could every say no. I sang at one person's funeral, and I sang at his daughter's wedding only a few short years earlier. It was hard, but very rewarding, and made me feel good that they thought enough of me to ask me to do it. With God's help I made it through the service with minimal tears, but it took a lot of strength. I have sung at funerals many times before, but never for a person who has lost their battle with the same disease that I was battling at the same time.

In my five plus years as a cancer patient, there have been thirty-six people, friends from our small community of only a little over a thousand people, that I know of who have been diagnosed with cancer. After I was diagnosed, and of those thirty-six, nineteen have already lost their battle with this horrible disease. Never take tomorrow for granted, accept life as a gift and enjoy it, and be thankful for the gift of tomorrow you have been given. I don't know why God has chosen me to continue to be the one to live. *Is there something He still wants me to do, or am I doing it, and He wants me to continue?* There goes those uncontrollable thoughts again.

Time has passed and I am still doing fine, treatment every three weeks is going well, still only a little tired the day after I have my treatment. My CTs are still looking good--no new tumors. I do know that once my cancer went metastatic, I will be on some kind of treatment for the rest of my life. If that is what I have to do to stay alive, that is what I will do, I can "live" with that. There have been times that I dream about going into hospice. What I would tell my children, grandchildren, sisters, brothers and people close to me? I know that seems morbid but it will happen, and I hope the words will come to me and I will know what to say and do to give them all comfort and help them celebrate my life, not mourn my death.

In 2020 the entire country was in an uproar there was a virus called Covid-19 that put the health of everyone in jeopardy. This pandemic has caused total havoc, businesses were closed for a period of time, face masks were worn by many, and there were protests and looting. Many people lost their lives for different reasons because of uncontrollable happenings. Medically high-risk people were afraid to leave their houses for fear of contracting the virus and possibly losing their lives. I know this because I was one of them. I spent most of my time at home doing things I put off for a long time, and a bit of time in the studio making jewelry, even though the craft fairs have been canceled this year because of Covid-19. When I did get out, my blood pressure would rise because I was apprehensive about being amongst people and possibly getting sick. I have been trying so hard to stay alive that I don't want this virus to take my life away from me. I am sure this too shall pass, and God will get us through this pandemic.

Today is the greatest day ever. It's the only day you have. Yesterday is gone. Tomorrow may not come. But this moment is yours. Won't you strive to feel great today? I have found this to be true and living life to its fullest has been the way I have tried to live my life, especially these last six years. Many people who are conflicted with cancer or any life-threatening disease ask— why me? I say, why not me, I am no better than anyone else, and I would never wish this disease on anyone. I have learned: play the hand that is dealt to you to the best of your ability, don't complain, be happy, and live like there is no tomorrow, because there may not be.

Next week, no one knows what will happen next week, I just know that "You never know how strong you are until being strong is the only choice you have." I also believe that "Faith is knowing you can fly, even if you don't have wings." Accept the gift of tomorrow that you are given.

Rivers never go in reverse,
so try to live like a river.
Forget your past and focus on your future.
Always be positive. Yesterday is gone,
live for today and thank God
for the gift of tomorrow.